# Contemplations of a Convert

# Contemplations of a Convert

KENNETH JOHNSON

DESERET BOOK
SALT LAKE CITY, UTAH

**Library of Congress Cataloging-in-Publication Data**

Johnson, Kenneth, 1940-

　　Contemplations of a convert / Kenneth Johnson.

　　p. cm.

　　Includes bibliographical references.

　　ISBN 1-57345-474-5 (hardcover)

　　1. Johnson, Kenneth, 1940-2. Church of Jesus Christ of Latter-day Saints–Biography. 3. Mormon converts– United States–Biography. I. Title.

BX8695.J645 A3 2000

289.3'092–dc21

[B]                                                                          99-086317

                                                                                    CIP

Printed in the United States of America                          72082-6555

10   9   8   7   6   5   4   3   2   1

# CONTENTS

# INTRODUCTION

Our society continues to drift farther and farther from the moorings of morality and the belief in divinity. Many human beings, not knowing their true identity and potential, search in vain for happiness in the pursuit of pleasure. Accumulating material things, they remain dissatisfied.

An experience I had as a young child demonstrates how the limitations of an unenlightened mind contribute to our naiveté. I recall sitting on the floor of our living room, amusing myself by repeatedly blowing up a balloon to the point that the rubber expanded so much that its green hue was barely discernible. Then I would release the air and blow up the balloon again. My enjoyment of doing so was suddenly shattered by a loud bang, which accompanied the disappearance of the balloon. I conducted a thorough search but could find the balloon nowhere. The pieces of shriveled rubber my mother produced as evidence of the demise of my plaything did not convince me. Given my limited childlike perspective, I couldn't imagine what had happened to my balloon, and I searched in vain for several days in the hope that it would magically reappear. Even offers of a replacement balloon did not console me. As a child, I was incapable of understanding that my toy had ceased to exist.

If our vision of life is limited to this mortal sphere, it is impossible to feel secure in the face of the many bursting balloons we encounter. Such experiences prompt us to ask, "Whom can we trust?" and "Where can we turn for peace and assurance?"

My heart resounds to the words of Ether, who declared, "Wherefore, whoso believeth in God might with surety hope for a better world, yea, even a place at the right hand of God, which hope cometh of faith, maketh an anchor to the souls of men, which would make them sure and steadfast, always abounding in good works, being led to glorify God" (Ether 12:4).

Belief in God gives purpose to life, and comprehension of the plan of salvation provides answers to otherwise unfathomable questions.

Such knowledge generates hope, which hope can develop into faith, furnishing an anchor to our souls and providing security through the stormy days of life. God the Eternal Father is the author of the plan. His Only Begotten Son, our Savior Jesus Christ, is the One who implemented that plan. Through Christ's sacrifice, the bands of death were broken and the door to immortality was opened.

Jesus Christ was a master teacher, and he used his parables to teach infinite truths in a way that they might be understood by finite minds.

My quest to understand his teachings has led me to analyze my personal experiences in the light of eternal principles. This book is a product of that pondering. I especially hope that those in their formative years of membership in the Church will find in these words encouragement and reason to continue in the faith. I will also be delighted if my insights contribute in some small way to strengthening families, particularly if those of the rising generation are motivated to set a course in life that will result in a "peace of conscience, because of [their] exceeding faith which they [have] in Jesus Christ" (Mosiah 4:3).

As a convert to The Church of Jesus Christ of Latter-day

Saints, I have discovered new insights and have acquired a new perspective on life. Learning that human beings are, in fact, children of God and, as such, eternal in nature, has made a tremendous difference in my life. Indeed, we cannot fully comprehend certain dimensions of our being unless we listen intently to the whisperings within that testify of our existence prior to mortal birth and of the certainty of life beyond the veil of death. My investigation of the truths of the gospel has opened to me an understanding of the sublime nature of the human soul. That understanding helps me to see things from a spiritual (eternal) perspective rather than from a temporal point of view. In this book, I attempt to share some of the insights I have acquired as a result of being taught the gospel. I have chosen to call these musings "contemplations of a convert," and I hope these thoughts and experiences will be helpful, especially to those who are only now discovering the truths of the restored gospel.

Like Nephi, I "labor diligently to write, to persuade our children, and also our brethren, to believe in Christ, and to be reconciled to God; for we know that it is by grace that we are saved, after all we can do" (2 Nephi 25:23).

Notwithstanding my limited capacity to express myself adequately, I hope readers will gain through these writings additional faith in gospel doctrines and principles that have been revealed in this latter-day dispensation. These truths have enabled me to view the bursting balloons of mortality from a broader perspective.

Explore in the following pages the continuing relevance, value, and power of the principles taught by the Savior during his mortal ministry and reaffirmed through living prophets in our day. I testify that adherence to these principles will result in the promised, two-fold reward: "even peace in this world, and eternal life in the world to come" (D&C 59:23).

# Autobiographical Insights

# AUTOBIOGRAPHICAL INSIGHTS

## A CHERISHED CHILDHOOD

Bertie Alfred Maurice Johnson married Ada Hutson on July 29, 1933. Those were difficult times of economic depression, and Bertie was unable to find employment, so in the early days of their married life Ada worked as a finisher in a shoe factory to support them financially. Bertie also obtained a position in the shoe manufacturing industry before being offered a position in the trades department of Reckitt and Colmans, where his father worked in the sawmill. Mastering the skill of erecting scaffolding, Bertie became well respected for his expertise in this field. I have often wondered how, under different circumstances and in more favorable times, he would have benefited from a wider sphere of opportunity and been able to use his talents to even greater effect.

He did, however, achieve outstanding success in the things that really matter. In 1937, a son, Clive, was born to Ada and Bertie; my birth followed in July 1940. World War II was underway, and on December 1 of that year, my father was ordered to report for military service in the British Army and was assigned to the Aldershot Training Barracks. He later served at Trimingham, Norfolk, where he was deployed with units assigned to coastal defenses before being transferred to the war zone in Italy. At the time of his discharge from active duty on January 26, 1946, his commanding officer noted in Bertie's release book that Bertie's military conduct had been exemplary. The commanding officer added these observations concerning Johnson, B. A.: "He has always been a willing and conscientious worker, is above average in intelligence, [and is] honest and sober in his habits." I am thrilled every time I read that description of the man I came to know as a wise and wonderful father.

During the years when our father was separated from us, Mother did remarkably well in ensuring my brother and me a happy young childhood. Similar accolades could be written of her parenting accomplishments.

Norwich, the city where we lived, is a cathedral city and was a prime target for German bombing raids. For a short period of time during the war, our family was evacuated to Kings Lynn in Norfolk. While living there I contracted a strain of viral jaundice and according to my mother's account was critically ill and unresponsive to medical treatment. The lady with whom we were lodging suggested a treatment that consisted of laying warm, moist pieces of flannel on my stomach, which my mother did, repeating the process many times. I eventually regained my health, but as a result of the infection I suffered from recurring periods of illness until I was fourteen years old.

## FAMILY FRATERNITY

Following his return from military service, Dad made up for missed time spent with his two boys by arranging numerous occasions for us to participate together in family activities. One unforgettable experience occurred when he decided to provide us with swimming instruction. The only nearby swimming facilities were actually sections of a nearby river, around which wooden fencing, a boardwalk, and changing cubicles had been erected. The best of these facilities was at Lakenham, Norwich. I vividly recall Dad taking my brother or me into the water while the other sat observing on the edge of the boardwalk at the side of the pool.

During one of our visits to the swimming pool, while Dad was working with Clive and I was watching, somebody pushed me from behind into the water. I dropped like a stone to the river bed and had the sensation of being surrounded by a large bubble. I was gasping for breath and seemed to rise to the surface and then submerge several times. As I sank to the bottom once more, a strong arm clasped me around my body and lifted me to the surface. An unknown onlooker had witnessed what had happened and had come to my rescue. This experience left an indelible impression on my mind, since it was quite possible to drift downstream from the swimming pool section unnoticed and not be discovered in time to prevent drowning.

As a boy, I attended the Thorpe Hamlet Infant and Junior schools. My recurring bouts of illness affected my academic development, and I did not initially pass the qualifying exam for entry into a grammar school at age eleven. I entered the first year of junior school while my brother was a fourth-year student. As with most schools, ours had a young man who liked to dominate all the other boys in his age group. During a break period while on the playground, the bully turned his attention to me and began to wrestle, trying to pull me to the ground. I retaliated and a fight developed. My brother and his classmates formed a ring around us and shouted words of encouragement to me. The teacher on duty stepped in and separated us, and we had to spend the remainder of the day sitting at the front of the class (in which my brother was a student) under the watchful eye of the headmaster. I may not have acted wisely, but the bully never bothered me again.

My brother was very patient with me, and we did many things together. For example, we would imitate knights of old. Using pieces of wood for swords, we would engage in mock combat. While Clive would try to emulate the flourish and artistry of a skilled swordsman, I would simply thrust my weapon directly at his body and claim victory. He was far from impressed by my direct style of combat. One Christmas we were each given a pair of boxing gloves as a gift. Because he was older and stronger, he could easily contain me, but my determined efforts to defeat him sometimes caused him to laugh so much that he could not defend himself.

## GROWING PAINS

Another memorable moment from my childhood involved a swarm of angry insects. I had seen cartoonists' depictions of what happens when a wasps' nest is disturbed, showing an unfortunate individual fleeing with a swarm of angry wasps in pursuit. This may not be a common occurrence, but we discovered that it really can happen. Clive and I and a friend were playing near our home in a wooded area known as Thorpe Woods. We were running among the trees when our friend leaped from a ledge of soil into a pile of dry leaves and landed in a wasps' nest. Although it was a frightening experience at the time, my brother and I have often laughed about it since, remembering the comic scene as we tried to outrun our angry assailants. We eventually arrived home, suffering from the discomfort of numerous wasp stings. I had wasps trapped in my curly hair, buzzing and desperately trying to free themselves. Tears rolled down my cheeks more because of fear than pain. Mother had to perform surgery on my hair with a pair of scissors to remove my unwelcome guests, but our friend suffered far greater consequences and had to receive medical treatment.

I encountered numerous health challenges during my childhood, including a full range of children's illnesses. I experienced the discomfort of measles, chicken pox, and scarlet fever. The latter condition required my confinement in the isolation wing of the hospital, where I had another memorable experience.

Each room contained two beds. The young man who occupied the other bed in my assigned room had almost recovered from his illness and was very energetic and mischievous. At the foot of the beds was a crank similar to those used to start the early models of motor vehicles. Rotating this handle in a clockwise direction would raise the bed; the reverse movement had the opposite effect. The range of movement was probably only about twelve inches, but my roommate convinced me that he could crush my body against the ceiling. To prove his point, he commenced to crank the bed upward. I must have expressed my fears in highly audible tones since a nurse came to investigate the cause of the commotion. Rescuing me from my assailant, she returned the bed to its original position and removed the young man from the room. I never saw him again and can only assume that, having completely recovered from the symptoms of scarlet fever, he was released from the hospital.

## ACTIVITIES AND EDUCATION

Mother was a member of the Church of England, and on many occasions expressed her concern that, because of the wartime conditions, I had never been christened or confirmed a member of that church.

My father had a good voice. He loved music and sang tenor in the Scot Memorial Methodist Choir. It was probably because of his influence that I submitted my name to play the part of the page in a musical rendering of "Good King Wenceslas" at the school Christmas concert. The words "Sire, he lives a good league hence, underneath the mountain: right against the forest fence, by Saint Agnus Fountain," still evoke fond memories. It was my first experience in "the world of entertainment."

At age thirteen I sat for the entrance examination to obtain a place at the Norwich City College. This resulted in an unforgettable event. One of the test papers involved reading an account of the first flight by the Wright brothers. Afterward, the paper was removed and replaced by a list of questions aimed at assessing how well the prospective student had comprehended the article. It was approximately three weeks after the examination that I was invited back to the college to meet with members of the examining panel. It was an intimidating experience to sit before this distinguished group and respond to their questions.

"Do you know anybody at the college?"

"No, my brother attended, but he is now continuing his education elsewhere and fulfilling a trade apprenticeship."

"Did you have any access to the test paper before taking the exam?"

I responded that I had not.

That was the vein of questioning to which I was subjected. Eventually the chairman of the board of examiners explained why they were conducting such an interview. Never in the history of the college had a student achieved a score of 100 percent on the questions contained in this paper. And I had.

The ability to retain salient facts in my mind and discard comparatively unimportant supportive information was a talent I had not previously recognized in myself or fully appreciated. This gift has since proved valuable in both my business and priesthood responsibilities, particularly as my native ability has been enhanced by the companionship of the Holy Spirit.

I qualified for a place at the college, and broader horizons of possibility opened up to me. My participation in a third-year college stage production proved to be a significant factor in my future activities. The art master who was directing the production knew of my painting aptitude and asked me to help paint the scenery. While I painted, I sang. Hearing my renditions, the master offered me a part in the production. It was only a minor part, but it provided me with an opportunity once again to perform in public and gain additional experience. The college had a tradition of staging a Christmas concert composed of a recital of classical music, which was greatly enjoyed by the teaching staff but merely tolerated by most of the students. As Christmas of 1955 approached, I was contacted by two fellow students who suggested that we participate together in the upcoming Christmas concert. One played the piano and the other the drums. I would be the vocalist. We performed at the concert after only two or three practices. I sang two songs: "Christmas Alphabet" and "Seventeen," both popular songs of that time. The response from the students was remarkable as they rose to their feet to applaud. I can only conclude that they appreciated the light relief provided by the contrast between our popular renditions and the heavier classical performances.

## INTROSPECTION AND PERSONAL DEVELOPMENT

When I left college in the summer of 1956, I commenced a printing apprenticeship. Not long after that I contracted an illness that caused me to experience blurred vision and severe headaches, which affected me over a period of several weeks. My condition was eventually diagnosed as nervous exhaustion.

Without my realizing it, making the transition from college life and adjusting to the demands of an unfamiliar environment had had a detrimental effect on my health. The pressure that caused the illness was selfimposed, and getting well required me to develop a greater degree of inner strength in order to overcome oppressive feelings that had encompassed me. As ever, my parents were extremely supportive during this period of personal challenge. Once I had recovered, I resumed my sporting activities and won a place on a local youth soccer team that had a record of winning the under-18 league championship and other trophies. This trend continued for the two years that I was a member of the team.

Toward the end of my sixteenth year, a friend I had known at college invited me to become the singer in a "skiffle group." (The group, consisting of guitars, tea chest bass, washboard, drums, and vocals, played upbeat versions of folk songs.) My brother loaned me £2.50 to use as a deposit on the purchase of an acoustic guitar. I quickly learned to play three chords, and thus equipped, I was sufficiently qualified to be a member of the group. By practicing and performing, we eventually achieved a level of musical competence that kept our group somewhat in demand.

During the same time, I also made a transition from the minor soccer league to playing in the East Anglian League for Thorpe St. Andrew, a team named after the geographical location of the sports ground where the team played. Soccer and music distracted from my studies, but I enjoyed the highlights and adulation they provided. At that time, I had no real direction or appreciation for the more important things of life.

## IMPORTANT EVENTS THAT WOULD AFFECT MY LIFE

In 1935, Evelyn Martins was introduced to The Church of Jesus Christ of Latter-day Saints by her brother Bert, who was dating and was later to marry Elsie Tuttle, who was a member of the Church. Evelyn was dating Thomas G. Wilson, and they began to attend Church meetings together. They were taught and baptized by Elder Leroy Kettle, who also subsequently performed their civil marriage ceremony.

The first child born to Evelyn and Thomas was a daughter, Pamela, who was raised in an environment of love and gospel light that resulted in her developing a deep faith in the Savior and a personal testimony of the restoration of the gospel. Following the dedication of the London Temple in September 1958, Thomas, Evelyn, Pamela, and her siblings, Margaret, Dean, and Susan, were sealed as a family on April 4, 1959.

## A FRESH VIEW

I met Pamela V. Wilson on April 11, 1959, at the Norman School of Dancing, and she shortly thereafter introduced me to the Church. Pamela's father, Thomas G. Wilson, baptized me on August 16, 1959, and her uncle, Bert W. Martins, confirmed me a member of the Church. As the light of the gospel began to illuminate my mind, my perception of myself and my understanding of the purpose of life was transformed. One of the effects of my newfound religion was that I immersed myself in the studies I had previously neglected and achieved remarkable results.

Pamela and I were married in March 1962 at the Norwich Chapel (60 Park Lane, Norwich), in a civil ceremony, which is required by British law. Though we weren't married in the temple at this time, we did spend our honeymoon at the London Temple, staying for one night at the Manor House on the temple grounds and for several nights at Edenbrook, then the temple's accommodation facility. We were later sealed in that temple on January 18, 1964.

My first Church calling was to serve as a counselor in the branch MIA superintendency. In September 1960 I was ordained to the office of elder in the Melchizedek Priesthood by Jeffrey F. Packe. I was called to serve as age-group counselor in the District MIA, and in 1962 Pamela and I were called to preside over the district Young Women and Young Men organization. Not long after that, I also received the call to serve as a counselor to Kenneth Warren in the branch presidency. Kenneth would later become my business partner. I continued to serve in these capacities until 1970.

## MARRIAGE COVENANTS

Just prior to our wedding, Pamela and I purchased some basic items of furniture, which the suppliers stored for us since we didn't yet have a home to move into. At this time, Pamela was working for G. F. Butchers Drapers. Mr. Leslie Butcher, the eldest of three brothers who owned the business, asked Pamela where we planned to live once we were married. That was not an unreasonable question, since the wedding date was a little more than two weeks away. Pamela responded that we were still looking for a home to rent. Mr. Butcher indicated that his wife had some properties and that he thought one was available for renting. The timing could not have been better, and the house at Number 14 Denmark Road, Norwich, became our first home with three bedrooms upstairs, and a lounge, living room, dining room, and small kitchen downstairs. The toilet was accessed only by an outside door adjacent to the kitchen. The house had no bath or shower facilities, but it was home.

Shortly after we returned from our honeymoon, it was announced that a special meeting was to be convened to discuss the building of a chapel to accommodate the Norwich Branch. It was an exciting experience to attend the meeting and to meet for the first time Elder Walt and Sister Ruth Stewart. Elder Stewart had been assigned to supervise the construction of the building, which would require volunteer labor provided by the members.

President Raymond Barber was serving as branch president, and two weeks after the meeting at which the chapel construction project was announced, he invited Pamela and me to meet with him following sacrament meeting. He asked if we were hoping to have a family. We looked at each other and then directed our attention to President Barber, conveying an affirmative response to what initially appeared to us to be an unusual question. He then proceeded to explain that one aspect of the building program then in place was to utilize the labor of building missionaries—young men who formed the basis of a work crew and who were called to do so without remuneration. (Ten shillings—about 75 cents—a week could not be defined as a wage.) Members of the local unit provided support and living accommodations for these young men, some as young as seventeen. We had space in our home, and President Barber wondered if we could provide accommodation for two of the four missionaries assigned to the project.

Yes, we were looking forward to having a family, but we had not anticipated having two teenage sons so soon after our marriage. The Lord had provided us with a home, not only to provide shelter for us but to share with others. Over the three-year period the chapel was under construction, Pamela and I enjoyed the companionship of a number of these young men. Elder Stewart was a great leader, and his outlook motivated me to write several songs ("The Labor Missionary Lament," "The LM Hop," "The Supervisor's Wife," and "When Our Mission's Over") to help boost the morale of the "labor missionaries," as they became known. One of the missionaries, Michael Corbishley, provided vocal harmony and Tom Ross and Dave Ellis also sang.

## CHURCH SERVICE AND CAREER OPPORTUNITIES

When Pamela and I were called to serve as district MIA leaders, President Jeffrey Packe suggested that we have Walt and Ruth Stewart serve as our counselors. What a learning opportunity that proved to be! The Stewarts had considerable experience and vision of what could and should be achieved. We were also blessed to have Ivan and Doreen Moss as counselors.

One of the highlights of the MIA program was an annual regional youth conference. Pamela and I adopted a "Come Follow Us" approach, and the youth enjoyed participating in sacred and secular vocal quartets, road shows, and sports and dance festivals.

We often remember with fondness our district-formation dance team, consisting of thirty-six couples dressed in costumes—black trousers and skirts and T-shirts dipped in yellow dye with crepe paper trimming—gliding across the dance floor to the rhythm of the cha-cha. Pamela had choreographed the performance to perfection, and our team was awarded first place in the competition. I was asked to write theme songs for the conferences, music and script for the road shows, and songs for youth quartets, all of which provided moments to remember. Margaret Wilson, the second eldest daughter of Thomas and Evelyn Wilson, has a lovely singing voice and was awarded first place in a popular music festival by singing "Mr. Right," a song I had composed for her. It was during that time and through those activities that I developed a warm and wonderful friendship with Colin Parker, a member of the Lowestoft Ward. We continue to be kindred spirits.

I completed my printing apprenticeship in 1961 and moved from the printing department of Reckitt and Colmans to become a letterpress machine minder at the Soman Wherry Press. Fourteen months later I was approached by the Norwich Engraving Company to join that firm as a process prover. Then, in 1963, Kenneth Warren asked me if I would be interested in joining him in a business venture as an insurance consultant. We agreed to become partners but decided that I would initially retain my current employment, devoting time in the evenings and on Saturdays to our insurance endeavors. In May 1964 I terminated my employment with the Norwich Engraving Company, and Kenneth and I launched Warren & Johnson as a registered company.

## THE MIRACLE OF BIRTH

The birth of our son, Kevin, in September 1966 brought Pamela and me closer to each other and to the Lord. He was born with some major physical challenges, and his poor health prompted our decision to visit Salt Lake City in January 1970. We were encouraged to do so by Dr. Dean Belnap, who was serving at that time as president of the London Mission. President Belnap was a medical doctor, who, after learning about Kevin's physical condition, advised us to seek medical advice at Primary Children's Hospital.

We had invested in our own home in the spring of 1969, a home that had been previously occupied by Dennis and Brenda Reeves and their family, located at 13 Sydney Road, Spixworth, on the outskirts of Norwich. In order to raise funds for our trip to Utah, we rented our home to a couple, sold our car and a typewriter, and borrowed some money from my parents. Kenneth Warren was left to manage the insurance business with the understanding that he should not concern himself with maintaining my interest in the business during my absence. The events, associations, and experiences we enjoyed while in Salt Lake City were faith promoting and led to Kevin later receiving the best possible medical care at the Great Ormond Street Hospital in London. We were so grateful for the hospitality of Lilly, Marjorie, and Bill Crotch, who had emigrated from our home town of Norwich many years earlier and who were friends of Pamela's parents. Without their help, we would not have been able to fulfill the purpose of our visit to Utah. Ron and Chris Coleby, whom we had previously known in England (he had served as the president of the Lowestoft Branch), also provided help in numerous ways.

## ECCLESIASTICAL, BUSINESS, AND FAMILY EXPERIENCES

After spending five months in Salt Lake City, we returned to England in May 1970. One week after our return, interviews were conducted in preparation for the creation of the East Anglia District by combining the Essex, Ipswich, and Norwich districts. Dennis Reeves was called to serve as district president, Jack Jacobs as first counselor, and I as second counselor. Elder Boyd K. Packer, newly called as a member of the Quorum of the Twelve Apostles, presided at the district conference and explained that the intent of this reorganization was to prepare for the ultimate creation of a stake. It was on this occasion that Brian Watling and I met for the first time. We developed a close association and became the best of friends. One year later, in June 1971, Elder Packer returned to England. Accompanied by Derek A. Cuthbert, who was serving as a regional representative, Elder Packer created the East Anglia Stake. Dennis Reeves was called to be president, Harold Hunt as first counselor, and I as second counselor.

These proved to be exciting years of learning and personal development for me. My business partner, Kenneth Warren, had done remarkably well in my absence. Working together, and with the Lord blessing us, our business continued to thrive. We had been frugal in the formative years of developing the business and were pleasantly surprised to learn that we could each draw a lump sum of money at the end of the financial year. Pamela, Kevin, and I held a family council to determine what would be the most prudent way to use this unexpected benefit.

At the time, our television projected only a monochrome picture, so we discussed replacing it with one that would provide a picture in color. Pam was in need of some better quality pots and pans for cooking, and we also considered how nice it would be to have a piano so that she could improve her playing ability and Kevin could take piano lessons. We decided that buying the pots and pans and a used piano would be the wisest way to expend the money. This proved to be an extremely good decision, and the items we purchased were of lasting worth to our family.

In February 1977, President Reeves was released, and I was

called to serve as stake president, a blessing that resulted in another period of personal refinement and provided a wonderful relationship with my excellent counselors, Brian Martin and Michael Fagg, two men whom I hold in high regard. The time I served in the stake presidency proved to be a special season of my life. During that period, I benefited from the tutelage of such pioneers of priesthood leadership in the British Isles as Derek Cuthbert, Joseph Hamstead, Peter Morley, Ian Swanney, Gordon Williams, and Arch Turvey.

In June 1977, my father died. Mum and Dad had been attending Church meetings, and a few weeks before his death, with Pamela providing the piano accompaniment, Dad, Kevin, and I had sung together "I Need Thee Every Hour" in a sacrament meeting. His passing left me with a great feeling of loss and disappointment that he had not participated in the ordinances of the gospel prior to his passing. Through the efforts of some wonderful sister missionaries, I was privileged to baptize my mother one year after Father's death.

My brother, Clive, was invited to undertake some work in the United States for government agencies, designing air conditioning and heating systems for hospitals. Eventually, he, his wife Janet, and their children, Teresa and Carl, moved to and settled in Medford, New Jersey.

In 1973, we expanded our business activities by purchasing a small instant printing company known as Gem Printing. This proved to be more demanding than anticipated, and between 1973 and 1976 I had to spend many hours supervising the work. In order to make possible the resale of the business and to honor customer orders, I moved the equipment into our home garage for several months prior to selling the company. I have often wondered how it was possible to convince the prospective buyer to purchase the company under such circumstances and in the process to receive in payment more than our original financial outlay. The business is still trading successfully. These business ventures had required many hours of hard work but had not detracted from family or Church service responsibilities.

In 1975, Elder Mark E. Petersen invited me to be present when he extended a call to Pamela's father, Thomas G. Wilson, to serve as a patriarch. Brother Wilson expressed his concerns about serving because of the condition of his health but willingly accepted. His ministry has since blessed many lives, and twenty-four years later he continues to be an influence for good. For me, the presence of seasoned members in our meetings brings a feeling of assurance and demonstrates a declaration of their faith.

## THE GOOD LIFE

The travel associated with my Church assignment often meant my leaving early Sunday morning and returning late Sunday evening. Pamela and Kevin would spend the day waiting for me at the meetinghouse. Our home in Spixworth was located nine miles from the Norwich Chapel, which is located at 19 Greenways, Eaton, and in 1976 we decided to move nearer the chapel. Given the price of real estate in this area, we had not previously been able to afford a home there. The years we resided in Spixworth had been excellent for our circumstances, as were the eight years we ended up residing in Eaton. In 1984 we moved again, this time to a rural area on the outskirts of Norwich known as East Carleton. This home offered the benefits of a small orchard, fruit cage (intended to protect the fruit from hungry birds), vegetable patch, and large glass house. In addition, the home was enhanced by an outdoor swimming pool and a lawn surrounded by flower beds. For the two years we lived in this location it was wonderfully refreshing to work in the garden, even though at times it was late in the evening and the shades of night had fallen before I would retire to repose in the comfort of our home. In order to keep the lawn trimmed and tidy, I would on occasion drive home from my office during the lunch period to cut the grass.

Eventually we decided that it would be prudent to move back into the city of Norwich to be closer to my mother and Pamela's parents. Although the upkeep of the garden of our home in the country imposed significant demands, it also provided me with many contemplative opportunities, which I regretted losing.

## ESTABLISHING THE CHURCH

In May 1978, Elders Gordon B. Hinckley and David B. Haight presided at a meeting held in the Royal Albert Hall, in which nine newly realigned stakes were organized. The stake over which I was to preside had fewer units and covered a smaller geographical area than it previously had. It was renamed the Norwich Stake. In 1983, Elder Haight returned to divide the Norwich Stake, creating the Ipswich Stake by including three units from adjoining stakes. Brian Watling, who had been serving as my counselor, was called to preside over the Ipswich Stake. I continued to serve as stake president until May 1986, when Elder Packer was assigned to reorganize the stake presidency.

My release marked the end of an era for me. I had enjoyed the mantle the Lord bestows upon those he calls to serve him, and I had enjoyed as well the remarkable priesthood and auxiliary leaders who had surrounded me and who won my deepest admiration. Their faith and dedication to establishing the Church in the area where they served had been exemplary. In addition to those previously mentioned, Christopher Freeman, Anthony Butcher, and Michael Peel are men with whom I served and for whom I have the greatest respect.

Because of difficulty finding musicians to provide suitable music for Church dances, we decided to form a family band.

Kevin provided keyboard accompaniment; Pamela's brother, Dean Wilson, played drums; Trevor Bidle, who is married to Pamela's sister Susan, and I played guitar and sang. Later, Alec Mitchell, a ward member, joined us to provide electric bass and vocal harmony. After playing together for several years, our final performance was at the Norwich Stake Valentine Dance in February 1990.

## LEARNING FROM LIFE'S CHALLENGES

September 1985 brought further opportunities for personal development. On an exceptionally busy day I had a number of pressing business appointments and was being besieged by clients requiring information and advice. Mother was not feeling well and called me before I left home for the office. I decided to visit her. That same morning, Kevin, who was working as a member of my staff, set out from home in his car, planning to pick up a friend on his way to the office.

Pamela accompanied me, and we tended to Mother's needs and arranged to call back later in the day. Arriving at the office, I was surprised that Kevin had not yet arrived but assumed he must have been delayed picking up his friend or been caught in traffic. I had been at my desk for about thirty minutes when I received a phone call from a nearby hospital. A nursing sister on duty in the emergency department advised me that Kevin had been involved in a motoring accident and said that she would call me back later with more information. As I placed the receiver back on its base, I sensed that the situation was more serious than had been conveyed in the telephone conversation, and I decided to go immediately to the hospital. I briefly explained to Pamela what had happened and then drove to the Norfolk & Norwich Hospital.

When I arrived, I found Kevin lying on a stretcher suspended on a gurney in the corridor of the hospital. He had a broken jaw and had suffered serious internal injuries. Shortly after I arrived he was taken to the intensive care unit. With nurses and doctors anxiously attending to and evaluating his condition, I asked if I could have a moment alone with him. I must have expressed my request in convincing tones because, after emphasizing the urgency of identifying the extent of Kevin's injuries, they agreed to briefly suspend their examination of him.

Alone in the hospital room with Kevin, I administered to him. This interlude did not take much time, but as I invited the hospital staff back into the room, the doctor explained that while they were waiting for me they had located a hospital file with information from a previous medical examination Kevin had received from a different doctor. That doctor was affiliated with the hospital but was working at another hospital that day. They telephoned him and described Kevin's symptoms. Based on his previous examination, the doctor surmised what was causing Kevin's internal bleeding. While Kevin was being prepared for surgery, the original doctor arrived at the hospital and helped to surgically repair Kevin's life-threatening injury.

The next day, when Pamela and I visited Kevin in his hospital room, he greeted us by saying, "It was the blessing that saved me!" That experience enhanced my appreciation for the power of the priesthood and the guidance of the Spirit, and it gave me a clearer vision of life's priorities. None of my business affairs suffered that day. I was able to satisfy the clients who were pressing me for attention and information, but, most importantly, I responded to the needs of my mother and our son. Whenever I sense that I am deviating from what is most important from an eternal perspective, my thoughts often return to the experiences of that day.

## THE JOY OF SERVICE

Following my release as stake president, I was blessed to serve as the ward gospel doctrine teacher and as a stake

institute teacher. The doctrines and principles I had come to
cherish prior to my call to serve in a stake presidency had
become of even greater worth to me. After a few weeks, I was
also called to serve as a counselor in the ward bishopric. Then,
in March 1987, I received a call to serve as a regional representative. My area of assignment was the north of England, many
miles from my home in Norwich. This call provided me the
opportunity to travel the highways of England and enjoy the
green, rolling hills of its beautiful countryside.

Kevin was then Elder Kevin Johnson serving in the Leeds
England Mission, one of the missions in my assigned area. For
many years, Pamela and her mother, Evelyn Wilson, had been
visiting teaching companions and continued as such, cycling
whenever possible to make their visits. Sister Wilson, in fact,
continued to cycle past the age of seventy. When necessary, I
would provide transportation, driving them to and from their
appointments. This gave me an opportunity to study the scriptures while waiting in the car for them to complete their visits.

Pamela has always taken an active role in the Church,
extending acts of compassionate service to elderly sisters in the
ward and serving at various times throughout our marriage as
ward Primary, Young Women, and Relief Society president and
as stake Primary president. She also served five years as a sem-
inary teacher while also teaching in Sunday School and in
women's auxiliaries. In addition, she directed our ward choir,
which was a very fulfilling experience for her.

In 1987, English Saints celebrated the sesquicentennial of
the gospel's arrival in the British Isles. It was a thrill to help
organize the associated activities and to realize as never before
the contributions made to the Church by the people of Great
Britain. Many of them left their homes in response to the call of
a prophet to settle in a new land, providing needed strength to
the heart of the Church.

I benefited greatly from my experiences in the northern regions of the country. In 1988 I was reassigned to the south of England.

I continued to play soccer and enjoyed participating in ward and stake five-a-side soccer competitions, particularly when Kevin and I were playing on the same team. But my soccer activity would later come to an abrupt end with my call to the Seventy.

## DEFENDING OUR FAITH

Kevin returned from full-time missionary service in 1988. Shortly after arriving home, he participated in auditions conducted by the BBC (British Broadcast Corporation) to identify a young adult member of the Church to appear in a television series titled *The A to Z of Religion*. A few days later he received a phone call informing him that he had been selected and that he would be required to travel to Belfast in Northern Ireland, where the program was produced. The caller informed him that one person could accompany him. I was delighted that he asked me to be his companion. On October 14, 1988, we traveled to London by car and boarded a flight from London's Heathrow Airport to Aldergrave Airport on the outskirts of Belfast.

The BBC staff entertained us throughout the day until 8:30 that night, when we were taken by car to a derelict warehouse. To get there, we traveled along the Crumlin and Falls Road, an area that previously had often been shown in television reports of terrorist activity in Northern Ireland. Arriving at the chosen location, our vehicle stopped outside a set of large metal gates. Our attention was captured by guard dogs excitedly barking and jumping against the barrier that separated them from the outside world. The animals had to be restrained before the gates could be opened for us to drive into a courtyard surrounding the building.

Kevin was ushered to a circle of light inside the darkened warehouse, while I was invited to join the technicians in a small cubicle located approximately twenty feet from where Kevin was standing. Having thought the interview would be conducted in a regular television studio, with Kevin facing the interviewer, I was shocked to see figures appear at the edge of the illuminated circle and commence to bombard Kevin with questions, apparently trying to disorient him. It was my impulse to run to his aid, but I soon realized how well Kevin was dealing with the situation.

The interrogation was relentless and lasted for one hour and fifteen minutes. Kevin later described the experience as being like a two-year mission condensed into seventy-five minutes. As distressing as it was to witness my son undergoing such an intense grilling, I was impressed by the courageous manner in which he responded and by the radiance of his countenance as he boldly declared his convictions.

The program was not aired until February 1989. We were all somewhat tense when we gathered as a family to view it. Kevin's anxiety was clearly evident. He had no control over what might have been selected from the extended interview for inclusion in the final, edited, 20-minute piece. We surmised the producers would not primarily be interested in promoting or clarifying the message of the Church; more likely, they would edit their piece to achieve maximum dramatic impact. Knowing he could not control the outcome, Kevin was understandably anxious.

But the many phone calls and the over 400 letters he received afterward reassured him that he had done well—particularly the letters from parents who were not of our faith but who commended Kevin for displaying qualities of character they said they desired in their own children. It was evidence that whenever you present truth and error side-by-side, the honest in heart recognize the truth. Kevin had defended his beliefs and represented his faith with commendable valor; as a result, several people were baptized and some members were influenced to return to Church activity.

## MOTHER'S PASSING

Mother had suffered a series of strokes and needed daily attention. I am grateful to have been able to care for her. Although my efforts were minuscule when compared with the time she devoted to me as a child, the care I gave her enhanced my feelings of appreciation for her. Pamela was magnificent in sitting with her, providing meals, taking care of household cleaning, washing clothes, brushing hair, and tending to every need. Eventually, Mother had to be admitted to a rest home and then to a hospital where she could be given constant professional care. On March 16, 1989, Pamela and I visited her at the East Dereham Hospital, where we found her content and at peace. Shortly after returning home, we received a phone call from a nursing sister advising us that Mum had passed peacefully away. One year later, when the London Temple reopened following extensive refurbishment, Pamela and I participated in the necessary ordinances in behalf of my parents. How sweet and satisfying is the doctrine of salvation for the dead at moments such as those.

## A CALL TO THE SEVENTY

In my capacity as a regional representative, I was invited to attend the Church's general conference in the spring of 1990. A phone call from President Gordon B. Hinckley a few days prior to my departure for Salt Lake City marked the opening of a new and totally unexpected chapter in my life. Following an interview and a call on March 29, 1990, to the Second Quorum of the Seventy, Pamela and I took a walk together. As we walked, I enumerated the many matters that required my attention in order to be available to serve. The long list could easily have been overwhelming. In the midst of my mental acrobatics, Pamela restored my tranquillity by saying, "As long as we are together, everything will be all right."

My name was presented for a sustaining vote at the Saturday afternoon session of general conference on March 31. Following the meeting, I enjoyed receiving many heartwarming, enthusiastic expressions of support from the regional representatives with whom I had served in the United Kingdom. When Pamela and I finally returned to our hotel following conference, I didn't have much time before having to set out for the Tabernacle for general priesthood meeting. As I was leaving the hotel room, I heard the telephone ring. I paused at the door to see who might be calling. Pamela called me back, indicating that a secretary to the First Presidency wished to speak with me. "I know how much your life has been disrupted this weekend," he said, "but I am calling to notify you that you have been assigned to speak for five minutes in tonight's meeting." I can't remember anything about the walk that night from the hotel to Temple Square.

We were separated from our family in England and could not advise them of my call until after it had been announced. We stayed up late that night in order to phone Kevin and share with him what had transpired. He expressed his support and encouragement. We wanted Kevin to inform Pamela's parents, rather than have them learn the news from somebody else as they arrived at church for Sunday meetings.

I was assigned to serve in the United Kingdom-Africa area presidency with Elder Jack H. Goaslind as president and Elder Robert E. Sackley as first counselor. These brethren helped me through those early days of accelerated learning. On Saturday, April 21, I accompanied Elder Sackley to Manchester for my first stake conference as a General Authority. Having spent almost all our lives in the same area of England, Pamela and I left our home in Norwich on May 21, moving to Solihull, where the area office was located. Leaving our comfortable surroundings and friends was for us a tender experience. But it did not take us long to settle, and we soon felt at home because of the friendly disposition of the area office staff and ward members.

## AREA PRESIDENCY ASSIGNMENTS

Elder Jeffrey R. Holland, then a member of the First Quorum of the Seventy, arrived in August 1990 to serve as area president, with his wife, Patricia, and their son, David. Elder Jack and Sister Gwen Goaslind returned to Salt Lake City. With the creation of the Africa Area Presidency in October 1990, Elder Robert Sackley was reassigned to serve in Africa, and Elder Gerald E. and Sister Evelyn Melchin joined the presidency of what was then the United Kingdom-Ireland Area. Those were exciting days, and we enjoyed an outpouring of inspiration as we assembled together in presidency meetings, traveled to meet with stake presidencies throughout the area, and conducted priesthood leadership meetings, promoting the theme "Lift Up Your Eyes" (John 4:35). It was difficult for me to imagine that Elder Jeffrey R. Holland, as a young full-time missionary, and I, a new convert, had sat together in the Norwich Chapel in 1960. Now we were serving together as General Authorities and members of an area presidency.

In May 1991, the United Kingdom-Ireland Area was expanded to include the Nordic countries: Finland, Sweden, Norway, Denmark, and Iceland. This expansion added a wonderful new dimension to my ministry. In these beautiful countries, the faithful Saints are unfailing in their devotion and dedication, though their growth in numbers has not been dynamic. My association with those with whom I served had, and continues to have, a refining and edifying influence in my life. What a thrill it is to serve with the Lord's anointed servants, not only to bask in the light of their understanding but to also gain a greater vision of a Christlike life through their example and application of gospel principles.

In August 1992 Elder Melchin was reassigned, and Elder Hugh W. Pinnock and his remarkable wife, Anne, joined us, and we served together as a presidency for one year. Then, while I was attending the April 1993 general conference in Salt Lake City, I received a message that I was to meet with President Thomas S. Monson. He called me to become a member of the First Quorum of Seventy and assigned me to serve as president of the Europe North Area with Elder Hugh W. Pinnock as first counselor and Elder Graham W. Doxey as second counselor. Elder and Sister Holland left England in August 1993, having made an indelible impression in our lives and in the hearts of the Saints they had so unselfishly served.

## FEELINGS OF INADEQUACY

I recall my impressions while traveling to the April 1993 general conference. By then, the intense feelings of inadequacy I had originally felt when called to serve as a General Authority had eased a little, and I no longer sat in meetings thinking someone would approach me and inquire as to what I was doing there and ask me to leave. On the return journey to England, I pondered the meetings I had attended and the instruction I had received. I concluded that in communicating with me, members of the First Presidency and Quorum of the Twelve Apostles were reaching down to the basic elements of their understanding while I was reaching up to the full extent of my capacity, and we were just barely making contact. How could I possibly fulfill my assignment to teach what I had been taught with the same spirit and power that I had experienced? I concluded that if I relied on the Lord, he would communicate his message according to his will, after all that I could do. That we continue to learn from those with whom we serve was a truth I realized over and over during the two years I served as president of the Europe North Area.

We had many spiritual highlights, but one never-to-be-forgotten experience was participating in the groundbreaking service for the Preston England Temple with President Gordon B. Hinckley presiding. Ten thousand Saints assembled on the rolling hills on the outskirts of Chorley for that historic event. President Hinckley had tender reunions with members he had associated with while serving as a young missionary in England. I expressed my feelings on that occasion by saying: "I foresee a new era. I see thousands of people accepting the truth and coming to this temple to enter into covenants with the Lord."

## FURTHERING OUR FAITH IN THE PHILIPPINES

The April 1995 general conference heralded another exciting challenge and opportunity for growth and personal development. During that week, Pamela and I were invited to meet with President James E. Faust. He informed us that commencing August 15, our assignment would be to serve in the Philippines-Micronesia Area Presidency with Elder Ben B. Banks as president. Filipino Elder Augusto A. Lim and I were called as his counselors. Pamela and I had little knowledge of those islands or the remarkable people who inhabit them. I had come to know Elder Lim when we were both serving as stake presidents in our native lands and through associating together at general conference meetings. Elder Banks had served as president of the Scotland Edinburgh Mission, and we had a common link in Elder Jack H. Goaslind, who had introduced us.

My understanding of how the gospel can impact lives for good increased dramatically in this assignment. Notwithstanding the cultural differences, it was reassuring to discover that the principles of the gospel are applicable and beneficial regardless of widely differing circumstances. Pamela and I had never before witnessed such poverty and were amazed to observe the faith and optimistic outlook of the Filipino people. Not only did we develop a great admiration for them, but we gained a greater appreciation for opportunities and amenities we had largely taken for granted throughout our lives. It is incredible to imagine that there was only one native Filipino member present at the military cemetery in Makati Manila in 1961 when Elder Gordon B. Hinckley prayed that the Lord would bless the land and people with the light of the everlasting gospel. When we arrived in the Philippines in 1995, the membership of the Church was approaching 400,000.

After serving for one year as a counselor to Elder Banks, I received the assignment to be the area president. Elder Lim was called to preside as the first Filipino president of the Manila Philippines Temple, and Elders Sheldon F. Child and Quentin E. Cook, newly called General Authorities, arrived to serve as counselors in the area presidency. Once more as we sought the will of the Lord, a wonderful outpouring of inspiration distilled upon us, and we were blessed with a united vision of what the Lord desired of us.

## PAMELA'S PATIENT PERSEVERANCE

In 1990, Pamela had a lens implanted in her right eye to restore her vision, which had been impaired by a cataract. Eight months later she had emergency surgery to repair the retina, which was detaching due to the lens-implant surgery. She underwent the same lens implant procedure for her left eye in May 1995 before we left England for the Philippines. In January 1997, Pamela began experiencing more retina problems with her right eye, and she consulted an ophthalmologist at the St. Luke's Hospital in Manila. Because the hospital lacked advanced knowledge and modern equipment, we obtained permission to leave our area and travel to the United States for treatment. Two additional attempts to repair the retina proved unsuccessful. Because Pamela needed to be under the care of the ophthalmologist who performed the surgeries in Salt Lake City, our assignment to the Philippines was terminated on June 1, 1997.

It was with feelings of regret that we concluded our service there. We had grown to love the people and had learned so much from them. It had been an honor to serve with them. Pamela emerged from this very difficult and prolonged period with an outlook and attitude that increased my already deep admiration of her courage and character.

## THE PATTERN OF REASSIGNMENT

For the first time since my call as a General Authority, I was assigned to a position at Church headquarters in Salt Lake City. Elder Lynn G. Robbins and I were called to serve as counselors to Elder Hugh W. Pinnock in the North America Central Area Presidency. Regular interaction with members of the Quorum of the Twelve Apostles provided me with many edifying and inspirational experiences and gave me an expanded vision of purpose and possibilities.

The North America Central Area extends from Denver in the west to Chicago in the east and from St. Louis on the south to the Northwest Territories in the far northern stretches of Canada. Serving in this broad area opened for me a new catalog of exciting opportunities, which evoked poignant feelings while walking where pioneers had walked, lived, and died. Their incomparable faith lives on, generating a sense of the sacred at locations where they toiled and suffered. Seeing these sites and reflecting on their heroic deeds added to our reservoir of inspirational experiences. We served together as a presidency for twelve months, and then Elder Robbins, who was competent in speaking Spanish, was reassigned to a post in South America.

Elder Yoshihiko Kikuchi joined us in the presidency of the North America Central Area. Each of the brethren with whom I have served has helped to expand my understanding and appreciation for the gospel and the benefits and blessings of diversity. Born and raised in different countries with differing backgrounds and perspectives, all are united in the cause of the gospel. Assignments will continue to change, as will the brethren with whom I have the privilege to serve. But one thing is sure: the process of personal refinement will continue.

## THE ETERNAL NATURE OF THE FAMILY

One of the significant blessings that accompanies a call as a General Authority is the authority to perform sealing ordinances in the House of the Lord. My appreciation for this sacred opportunity was enhanced on April 3, 1998, when I was overwhelmed by feelings of gratitude to perform the ordinance of eternal marriage for Kevin and his sweetheart, Joanne, in the Salt Lake Temple. Surrounded on that occasion by cherished friends and loved ones, we enjoyed an incomparable tender moment of reverent reflection.

Kevin was by then established in his career, developing management-training programs and directing seminars for business executives and staff members. His Church service has included callings as a counselor in a bishopric and as a member of a stake high council.

The culmination of the divine doctrines taught by the Savior is found in the establishment of eternal family units. Families are an integral part of the greatest of all the gifts of God—eternal life. As I ponder these principles, I am filled with the desire to comply with the requirements necessary to attain the promised blessings. I have implicit faith in the necessity of participating in the ordinances of baptism, confirmation, priesthood ordination, and temple ordinances, culminating in the covenant of eternal marriage. I also recognize that unless we make and keep sacred covenants, these outward evidences of our faith are not fully satisfactory, since without our full commitment, the Holy Spirit of Promise cannot attend or ratify our actions. When fathers lovingly preside and provide, and devoted mothers tutor and nurture, children in such a family have the optimum chance of reaching their physical and spiritual potential, developing self-discipline and understanding individual responsibility.

When this divinely appointed pattern of parenting and family relationships is followed, unity, harmony, and love result, and the home becomes a place where parents and children, sealed as an eternal family, enjoy being together and serving one another. Individuals from such homes make invaluable contributions to the Church and to the society in which they live.

## PERSONAL REFLECTIONS

Throughout my life I have enjoyed association with and the companionship of exceptional people, whether in my family, Church associations, business dealings, or our circle of valued friends. Each individual has woven a beautiful thread into the fabric of my being. Their thoughtfulness, encouragement, and examples have motivated me to try harder to be better. The list of names is too numerous to compile, but the impact of their influence is forever embedded in my heart. I am so grateful to my Father in Heaven for encompassing me in such an extraordinary circle of love and sociality.

# PART ONE

## Lessons Learned

# WE ALL HAVE
# A FATHER IN WHOM
# WE CAN TRUST

## "DAD'S COMING HOME!"

At the time of my birth, the clouds of World War II over-shadowed Europe and were sweeping across the English Channel to the British coastline. My father, like thousands of other men of his generation, was required to report for active military service. My elder brother and I were shielded from much of the turmoil and fear that surrounded us by a mother who compensated for the absence of our father by involving us in a variety of activities. I learned that when fathers are absent, mothers can be the recipients of compensatory blessings. I have fond memories of those days and, without fully under-standing who my father was or what he was doing, I recall my mother speaking of her beloved companion as she received letters from him.

My first recollection of meeting my father was when I was five years old. A telegram had been delivered to our home, and my mother stood with the gold-colored envelope in her hand, making no attempt to open it. I did not realize then as I do now the reason she hesitated and the message it might have contained. Eventually, and with great difficulty, she fumbled with the flap of the envelope. This seemed to take a long time. Mother read the telegram but had no immediate response. Finally, raising the telegram high above her head, she joyfully exclaimed, "Dad's coming home! Dad's coming home!"

Holding the telegram high in the air and with a skipping step, Mother set out to share the news with my father's parents, who lived in the house adjoining ours. "Dad's coming home! Dad's coming home!" she shouted. My brother followed close behind, shouting, "Dad's coming home! Dad's coming home!" I brought up the rear, also shouting, "Dad's coming home! Dad's coming home!" while inwardly wondering, "Who's Dad?"

The next morning when I awoke, a man I didn't know was sitting on the edge of my bed holding a leather soccer ball he'd brought from Italy. He asked if my brother and I would like to play soccer with him. Somewhat hesitantly, I agreed, and we went to an area of grassland near our home to play. This was the beginning of my father's continuing influence in my life. After getting to know him, I wanted to spend every moment that I could in his company.

## HELPING DAD IN HIS WORKSHOP

We lived, as did many others in those war-torn years, in humble circumstances. Our house was modestly furnished, but Dad had many skills and used them to beautify our home. He raised the Anderson air-raid shelter in our garden to ground level and made it his workshop. He spent many hours there, repairing shoes and making furniture for our home. It was my particular pleasure to wander into this workshop and watch him. Just to be in his presence was a thrill. When he invited me to help him by passing him a hammer, a screwdriver, or some other tool, I was convinced that my help was necessary and that without me he would not be able to complete his task.

Using a variety of pieces of wood obtained from different sources and considered by others to be unsuitable for any practical use, he created items of great beauty and worth for our family. As he worked, he would play a game with me, inviting me to discover what he was making. I was seldom able to do so until the components were completed and the object assembled. Then I would excitedly exclaim, "It's a bookcase!" or "It's a table!" and wonder at his ability to create so much from so little.

## SERVICE DRAWS US CLOSER TO GOD

As I reflect upon these wonderful memories, I realize that my father did not need my help to complete his work. I was the beneficiary of his invitation to help, and through these experiences I came to know him and love him.

In our association with our Heavenly Father, we believe that the service we engage in is for *his* benefit, when in reality the little help we render is comparable to my handing tools to my father. When we give service, the relationship that develops between us and our Maker is of greater significance than the contribution we make. As expressed by King Benjamin, "For how knoweth a man the master whom he has not served, and who is a stranger unto him, and is far from the thoughts and intents of his heart?" (Mosiah 5:13).

Just as I was not able to fully comprehend what my earthly father was building until he completed his work, so it is with our relationship to the work of our Heavenly Father. When his kingdom is established and the work is completed, we will recognize our home and shout for joy.

## SERVICE IS ESSENTIAL FOR A HAPPY LIFE

Selfless service is an essential ingredient of a full and happy life. President Marion G. Romney said in this regard:

"Service is not something we endure on this earth so we can earn the right to live in the celestial kingdom. Service is the very fiber of which an exalted life in the Celestial Kingdom is made" (in Conference Report, October 1982, 135; or *Ensign*, November 1982, 93).

Obtaining a place in the celestial kingdom is not comparable to being allocated a seat in the audience of a consummate concert. Rather, it will involve our playing in the orchestra.

We do not need to know the answer to every question or comprehend the reason for every challenge we face in order to feel secure in the knowledge of our divine Creator. In the words of Nephi, "I know that he loveth his children; nevertheless, I do not know the meaning of all things" (1 Nephi 11:17).

Reflecting on my experiences with my father and the lessons he taught me has enabled me to develop a greater appreciation for my Heavenly Father.

## LESSONS IN LEARNING

As I grew older, the teaching continued. I vividly recall the day my father taught me to use a handsaw. He positioned a piece of wood so that it extended eight inches beyond the edge of the workbench. He then clamped it in place with a bench vice. He then marked with his pencil a six-inch piece of wood. He invited me to cut the wood along the pencil line. At first I had difficulty maintaining control, and the teeth of the saw gouged marks on either side of the line until the saw blade eventually settled in the right place. I then proceeded to cut the wood, exerting all my energy to do so. It proved to be a demanding task, requiring a considerable period of time for me to complete the cut. My father then clamped another piece of wood in the vice and proceeded to demonstrate how one could, using the full length of the blade and relatively little effort, efficiently cut the wood into the required lengths. My father's skill was the product of many years of practice, and I realized it would take time and numerous attempts before I could match his level of mastery.

I recall learning to drive a car under the watchful eye of my driving instructor. During the early lessons I concluded that it would be impossible to implement all that he required of me. I was convinced that no one could coordinate all the procedures described and still maintain control of the vehicle. But after receiving continued coaching and repeatedly practicing maneuvers, I was finally able to do so.

I am reminded of the statement of Ralph Waldo Emerson, "That which we persist in doing becomes easier to do. Not that the nature of the thing itself changes, but the power to do it is increased."

This principle is so relevant to our Church service opportunities. The source of our training is the Lord and his servants. The more we serve, the greater becomes our capacity to serve. The tender words of Alma to his son Helaman provide hope for all of us: "And now, O my son Helaman, behold, thou art in thy youth, and therefore, I beseech of thee that thou wilt hear my words and learn of me; for I do know that whosoever shall put their trust in God shall be supported in their trials, and their troubles, and their afflictions, and shall be lifted up at the last day" (Alma 36:3).

Imagine the day when we might be lifted above the clouds of confusion, be freed from the constriction and constraints of disbelief and disillusionment, and be capable of caring for and lifting others by virtue of our willing deference to divine direction.

## DIVINE INSIGHTS

The Savior acknowledged the source of his knowledge in these words, "The Son can do nothing of himself, but what he seeth the Father do" (John 5:19) and "I do nothing of myself;

but as my Father hath taught me, I speak these things" (John 8:28).

We develop a special affinity for those whom we serve, and we enjoy a closeness with those who devote time to teaching us. The Savior declared, "I love the father" (John 14:31), thereby disclosing the bond that exists between the Father and the Son.

These examples of the relationship between the Father and the Son recorded in holy scripture provide a wonderful insight into the potential for family love that exists in mortality. The account of Jesus' baptism in Matthew 3:17 reveals that the Father's voice was heard, declaring, "This is my beloved Son, in whom I am well pleased." I am so grateful to be able to genuinely join with children in singing the words, "I Know Heavenly Father Loves Me" (*Children's Songbook*, 228-29). The joy derived from mortal experiences provides patterns and promises of things eternal.

## THE GIFT OF RESURRECTION

Because of the Savior's redemptive work, death is not a destination to be feared; it is instead an experience to be anticipated and the means by which we obtain a fullness of joy. This would not be possible without the gift of resurrection. This truth is confirmed in holy writ in these words: "And the spirit and the body are the soul of man. And the resurrection from the dead is the redemption of the soul" (D&C 88:15-16). Further, "For man is spirit. The elements are eternal, and spirit and element, inseparably connected, receive a fulness of joy" (D&C 93:33). Is this joy made possible simply because we continue to live beyond the veil of death? I do not believe so. It is my conviction that the rejoicing results from reunion with our Heavenly Father and others who are dear to us. This is the power and the purpose of the gospel plan.

What assurance, what comfort, what peace results when

we comprehend the true nature and extent of our existence. Could this knowledge be the key to that which the Savior referred to as "the peace of God, which passeth all understanding"? (Philippians 4:7).

## THE ETIQUETTE AND ATTITUDE OF PRAYER

Joseph Smith taught that "the first principle of the gospel is to know for a certainty the character of God and to know that we can converse with Him as one man converseth with another" (*Teachings of the Prophet Joseph Smith*, 345).

Statements under the heading of *Prayer* in the Bible Dictionary reflect my thoughts: "As soon as we learn the true relationship in which we stand toward God (namely, God is our Father, and we are his children), then at once prayer becomes natural and instinctive on our part." It is our nature to wish to confer with those we love—to express concerns, to receive guidance, and to share feelings.

The Savior demonstrated the protocol of prayer by the reverence he used in addressing the Father in terms of "thee, thy, thine, and thou." Note also the tenor of his expressions, which were not directing or demanding but rather inquiring and deferring. Returning to the Bible Dictionary, I resonate to the wisdom of these words: "Prayer is the act by which the will of the Father and the will of the child are brought into correspondence with each other. The object of prayer is not to change the will of God, but to secure for ourselves and for others blessings that God is already willing to grant, but that are made conditional on our asking for them." These thoughts so eloquently expressed convey the potency and purpose of prayer.

With the benefit of deeper understanding, I have found that my prayers for personal consideration, enhanced ability, or increased wisdom are more fulfilling when they are linked to the needs of others.

The following scriptural account emphatically illustrates this concept: "And the Lord said unto me: John, my beloved, what desirest thou? For if you shall ask what you will, it shall be granted unto you. And I said unto him: Lord, give unto me power over death." Although this is not an inappropriate request, his reason for asking reveals unusual devotion and remarkable vision: "That I may live and bring souls unto thee" (D&C 7:1-2). It requires a magnanimous individual to seek blessings in order to bless the lives of others and not for personal benefit.

Joseph Smith demonstrated this admirable characteristic while he was wrongfully incarcerated in Liberty Jail. As difficult and deplorable as were his own circumstances, he pleaded with the Lord not for his own relief but for that of the Saints: "Remember thy suffering saints, O our God; and thy servants will rejoice in thy name forever" (D&C 121:6). The Prophet's plea was followed by a remarkable revelation and words of comfort.

Jacob, a great prophet teacher, expresses a further example of this concept with this inspired insight: "But before ye seek for riches, seek ye for the kingdom of God. And after ye have obtained a hope in Christ ye shall obtain riches, if ye seek them; and ye will seek them for the intent to do good—to clothe the naked, and to feed the hungry, and to liberate the captive, and administer relief to the sick and the afflicted" (Jacob 2:18-19).

When we recognize the Lord's hand in all things, we become more generous in sharing the gifts we receive from him. We can all give something. In the words of Elder Jeffrey R. Holland, "We can give time if we don't have money, and we can give love when our time runs out" (*Ensign,* May 1996, 31).

## THY WILL, NOT MINE

These qualities are products of humility, evidenced by willing submission to the Lord. Nephi, the son of Helaman, is a perfect example of such submission. He received this remarkable praise from a voice from Heaven: "Blessed art thou, Nephi, for those things which thou hast done; for I have beheld how thou hast with unwearyingness declared the word, which I have given unto thee, unto this people. And thou hast not feared them, and hast not sought thine own life, *but hast sought my will,* and to keep my commandments. And now, because thou hast done this with such unwearyingness, behold, I will bless thee forever; and I will make thee mighty in word and in deed, in faith and in works; yea, even that all things shall be done unto thee according to thy word, *for thou shalt not ask that which is contrary to my will"* (Helaman 10:4-5; emphasis added).

To attune our thoughts fully to the Lord's thoughts is the ultimate expression of discipleship.

We are instructed in the scriptures to "hearken unto the Spirit which teacheth a man to pray" (2 Nephi 32:8). It is my conviction that the Spirit will also teach us *how* to pray, that through the process of pondering we can enjoy enlightenment and experience assurance. With all the technological achievements of our day, prayer remains and always will be the most advanced means of communication. We need no equipment or wires to make contact. We need only have faith in God as our Heavenly Father. That faith provides the key to understanding his true character. The Prophet Joseph Smith clarified and verified this principle when he said, "The knowledge that God exists, a correct understanding of His character, and a reassurance that He approves of one's conduct can help one's faith become perfect and fruitful abounding in righteousness" (*Lectures on Faith,* 65-66).

## KNOWING THE FATHER AND THE SON

On difficult days and during miserable moments, we should always remember that regardless of our circumstances, we all have a Father in whom we can trust and to whom we can turn for comfort and counsel. He is our Heavenly Father. What a thrill it is to hear children singing with conviction, "I am a child of God." We are in truth his offspring, and he is "not far from every one of us" (Acts 17:27).

You might justifiably ask how I can speak with such assurance about principles as profound as these. My response is the same as that of the Apostle Paul in Romans 8:16, "The Spirit itself beareth witness with our spirit, that we are the children of God."

Each day I enjoy an increased appreciation for the words of the Savior expressed in his great intercessory prayer: "And this is life eternal, that they might know thee the only true God, and Jesus Christ, whom thou hast sent" (John 17:3).

I know that he lives. I know that he loves us, for we are his children. His son, Jesus Christ, is our advocate with the Father and leads his Church today through living prophets. I testify that their words will guide us safely home.

# INDIVIDUAL
# RESPONSIBILITY

## RESPONSIBILITY FOR ACTIONS

Though they were not Latter-day Saints, my parents instilled in me a belief in and a respect for Christian values, which have developed into a firm foundation of faith. My brother and I were taught to honor the Sabbath by being sent to Sunday morning services at the local church, by being expected to wear our "Sunday best clothes," and by refraining from activities that were not in harmony with the intended nature of the day.

When I was seven or eight years old, my parents purchased a suit for me to wear on Sundays and for important occasions. It was the first time that I can remember recognizing the relationship between what we wear, how we feel, and the things we do. Wearing the suit influenced my behavior and reminded me of the significance of that special day.

On one occasion, however, my boyish enthusiasm dominated all other considerations. One of the activities we enjoyed on Sunday afternoon was walking through a wooded area known as Mousehold Heath. Gravel paths meandered there among bramble bushes, fern patches, and trees of different varieties. One Sunday afternoon my brother, a friend, and I were walking through this woodland enjoying the beauty that surrounded us. We were in an area of tall pine trees adjacent to a dirt road called Valley Drive when the friend looked up and spied a bird's nest high in the branches of one of the trees. A discussion ensued as to what species of bird might reside there and the possibility that the nest might contain eggs. We continued to review the possibilities until someone suggested that there was only one way to resolve the matter. One of us would have to climb the tree and look into the nest. This would not only confirm whether there were any eggs, but by their color and pattern reveal the type of bird.

My brother and our friend knew of only one person capable of such a task. They both looked at me, expressing their admiration of my ability to climb trees, however difficult a feat that might be.

Acknowledging their observations of my prowess, I commenced the difficult climb. The bark was slippery and brittle, and as I ascended, fragments broke away from the trunk of the tree. In places, sap was oozing to the surface of the bark, providing a beautiful aroma but forming a sticky coating. With fragments of broken bark showering on me from the branches above, I continued to climb, driven by a compulsion to satisfy our curiosity. I had no desire to disturb the nest or damage the contents, so I approached cautiously along a branch that would enable me to observe the interior without endangering the nest or any eggs that it might contain.

After a difficult ascent, I achieved my objective. However, looking down into a neatly woven basket of twigs and moss, I was disappointed to discover that there were no eggs and concluded that the nest had probably not been occupied for some time, possibly years. I communicated my findings to my companions below, then made my way back to the trunk of the tree and commenced my descent, renegotiating the obstacles I had encountered on the way up.

## FACING REALITY

It was only upon reaching the ground that the full realization of what I had done dawned on me. I had climbed the tree in my Sunday suit, and it was soiled with sap stains and black smudges of bark residue. The events that followed are indelibly etched in my memory. As I stood in the kitchen of our home trying to sponge the marks from my suit, my father stood beside me, explaining the gravity of my mistake. It was the only occasion I recall when he used "the laying on of hands" to teach me a principle. When I protested my innocence by saying, "But Clive made me do it," my father responded, "You are responsible for your own actions." Then he provided a vivid physical endorsement to help memorialize the message.

I still regret much about that moment, but I shall be ever grateful for the lesson learned, since the principle taught is not restricted to tree climbing or other boyhood escapades—we are *always* responsible for our own actions.

## CLEANSING AND SELF-WORTH

We removed the stains from my clothing using soap, water, and effort. More significant stains, usually not apparent to the physical eye, are much more difficult to remove. They are the stains left on our souls by acts of dishonesty, immorality, or other unseemly or unworthy behavior. Mercifully, the stains left by our sins can be removed by sincere repentance through the atonement of Christ and the grace of God. I was so relieved to find that the marks could be removed from my clothing. How much more comforting it is to know that the scars left by transgression can be erased from our souls and that we can be cleansed.

As a result of my experience in climbing the tree, I learned lessons that have had a lasting influence in my life. I determined never again to repeat such an activity unless appropriately dressed. Beyond that, feelings of self-respect stirred in me, causing me to take a greater interest in my personal appearance and to take better care of items entrusted to my keeping. Over time, I learned to appreciate the value of keeping clean such things as motor vehicles, the home, and the workplace. A sense of the importance of these things gradually expanded to encompass a greater respect for people and their possessions, and an appreciation for the inalienable right of freedom and the edifying essence of dignity. Such attitudes are the foundation of a wholesome, productive Christian lifestyle.

## MOTIVATION FOR SELF-IMPROVEMENT

Recognizing our responsibilities encourages us to try harder to become better individuals and citizens. Many, if not all, of us have at times felt inclined to relax, believing that mediocrity would somehow relieve us of the pressure imposed by responsibility. I have not found this to be so. The quest for self-improvement strengthens my desire to extend myself—not to be better than another but to become my best self. Rather than deter me, unsuccessful efforts have motivated me to evaluate why I did not accomplish what I set out to do and to try again.

Maturity gained over the years as a result of experience has brought me a greater degree of wisdom than that which I possessed as a youth. I have learned that unless we comply with the basic laws of physics, follow parental guidelines, and maintain a certain standard of honor and integrity, our potential for real progress is limited. One of the perils of living in mortality is our inability to immediately discern the effects of disobeying divine laws. Not seeing the consequences, many tend to dismiss God's laws as irrelevant. Many assume that he does not take note of or care what we do, and they foolishly decide to simply "eat, drink, and be merry" (2 Nephi 28:8)—a course that inevitably leads to dissatisfaction, unhappiness, poor health, and moral bankruptcy. Such people adhere to the "Korihor" philosophy, which was an assumption "that there could be no atonement made for the sins of men, but every man fared in this life according to the management of the creature; therefore every man prospered according to his genius, and that every man conquered according to his strength; and whatsoever a man did was no crime" (Alma 30:17).

In my experience, joy and purposeful living result when we view life from the perspective of unalterable truths and as a part of an eternal plan. Just as a contractor supervising a construction project begins with a framework upon which the external features of the building can be affixed, so we need to develop a foundation of faith and a reservoir of virtues. This substructure in human development is called character. Developing these concepts into the sphere of spiritual absolutes has been very enlightening.

## PRINCIPLES APPLIED

Discovering that I could solve a dilemma or decide on a course of action by applying principles was like turning on a light in a darkened room. Whenever a question arises, I now ponder until I can determine which gospel principle applies to the subject in question. This is the method the Lord has given to us: "And again, the elders, priests and teachers of this church shall teach the principles of my gospel, which are in the Bible and the Book of Mormon, in the which is the fulness of the gospel. And they shall observe the covenants and church articles to do them, and these shall be their teachings, as they shall be directed by the Spirit" (D&C 42:12-13). I have found this approach to be invaluable in responding to the complexities that encroach upon humankind. The principles of the restored gospel of Jesus Christ brought to me an expanded vision of "things as they really are" (Jacob 4:13), clarifying previous misconceptions and provoking further consideration. An experience I had in college illustrates this process.

## THE POWER TO CHOOSE

In my first year of studies at Norwich City College, I attained the highest marks in my class in art and geography. But in the second year in these subjects, I ranked thirtieth out of thirty-two students. The third year, I repeated my achievements of the first year. Since the same teacher gave instructions in art and geography to the first- and third-year students, I attributed the difference in my performance to the quality of the teacher. The thought of any other possibility never entered my mind. But with the light of understanding that accompanies an acceptance and application of gospel principles, I have since come to realize that my various levels of performance did not result from those who taught me. The difference in my achievement was more directly related to my motivation and determination to overcome obstacles—whether real or imagined. In the end, I had the capacity to do well or poorly and was responsible for my own success or failure. In this regard, the words of John Oxenham are of particular relevance. Consider with me the implications.

> *To every man there openeth a way and ways and a way.*
> *The high soul climbs the high way*
> *The low soul gropes the low*
> *And in between on the misty flats the rest drift to and fro*
> *To every man there openeth a high way and a low*
> *And every man decideth the way his soul shall go.*

Until I was exposed to the principles of the restored gospel, my circumstances were comparable to being "in between on the misty flats" drifting to and fro, possessing no real direction or long-term perception of the possibilities. My life provides evidence of the power we have to change. I am convinced that the greatest capacity for change within us is a recognition of who we really are and what we are capable of becoming as children of God.

## CHOOSE FOR THYSELF

The instructions given to Adam in the Garden of Eden included this statement: "Nevertheless, thou mayest choose for thyself, for it is given unto thee" (Moses 3:17). This ability to choose is "the agency of man" (Moses 4:3). This principle is further defined in the Book of Mormon: "Wherefore, men are free according to the flesh; and all things are given them which are expedient unto man. And they are free to choose liberty and eternal life, through the great Mediator of all men, or to choose captivity and death, according to the captivity and power of the devil; for he seeketh that all men might be miserable like unto himself" (2 Nephi 2:27).

## REALIZATION AND REMORSE

The anguish of Jacob Marley expressed in *A Christmas Carol* by Charles Dickens provides a poignant reminder to all of us of the possibility of missing the purpose and potential of life. Contemplate Marley's remorse as he discovers too late what could have been: "Not to know that any Christian spirit working kindly in its little sphere, whatever it may be, will find its mortal life too short for its vast means of usefulness. Not to know that no space of regret can make amends for one life's opportunities misused! Yet such was I! Oh! Such was I!"

Recognizing that life has a purpose and realizing the capacity we all have to chart a course provide motivation and direction as we confront difficult circumstances. The scriptures declare that the ultimate objective of this life is "to prepare to meet God" (Alma 34:32). To reach our destination, only to discover we have missed the purpose of the journey, would be devastating.

In the poem "Maud Muller" by John Greenleaf Whittier, we are reminded of this possibility in the familiar lines:

> *For of all sad words of tongue or pen,*
> *The saddest are these: "It might have been!"*

## MORAL AGENCY

Agency, the freedom to choose, is central to the plan of salvation. When options are presented, decisions have to be made, and consequences must follow. It was my choice to climb the tree; I was not compelled to do so. As a result, my clothing was soiled, and I had to face the consequences. Blaming the teacher for my poor performance was an evasion of the truth and my way of excusing myself from reality. We each make decisions and determine how we will respond to people and circumstances. Many of the restrictions in our lives are self-imposed. Over the years I have gained a greater appreciation for my father's penetrating statement of truth: "You are responsible for your own actions."

Recognizing and understanding the correct application of this principle is vital to our discovering our destiny and fulfilling our divine potential. When it comes to eternal opportunities, our decisions take on even greater significance. We cannot evade the consequences of our actions or avoid the fact that we are accountable for the choices we make. The clearest affirmation of this eternal truth, which I believe, is found in D&C 101:78: "Every man may act in doctrine and principle pertaining to futurity, according to the moral agency which I have given unto him, that every man may be accountable for his own sins in the day of judgment." Could there be a clearer statement of the truth that we are all responsible for our own actions? We rise to greater heights of achievement and personal fulfillment when we discover our divine heritage, which enables us to ascend above the mundane and mediocre things of life that can so easily cloud the unenlightened mind. Imagine the difference it makes when we are able to glimpse the glories of eternity. Freedom results from comprehending and complying with proven principles and eternal laws, not battling against them. These insights and associated ideals resulted from the realization that I was responsible for my own actions!

# LEARNING TO BE LED
# BY THE SPIRIT

## THE MOTORCYCLE RIDE

As a young man after completing college, I commenced a printing apprenticeship. In the early days of that endeavor, I associated with a fellow student who was fascinated by motorcycles. He initially purchased a low-powered machine but eventually replaced it with one that was larger and more powerful. Ultimately, he upgraded to a British-made AJS 350—a handsome machine painted black with gold trim. He enjoyed experimenting with the mechanical functions to improve performance by modifying and fine-tuning the engine.

One beautiful, sunny summer's day, my friend invited me to take a ride on the back of his motorcycle. It promised to be a pleasant diversion, and I readily accepted his invitation. Laws requiring the wearing of a helmet and protective clothing had not yet been introduced in Britain, so I mounted the passenger seat clad only in light clothing appropriate for a warm summer's day. With me seated behind my friend, we proceeded at first at a modest speed with my colleague coaching me how to lean to help negotiate a turn. Riding in the open air, weaving effortlessly through the streets of Norwich, was an enjoyable experience.

Eventually, we ascended Ketts Hill, drove through a residential area, then entered more open country and a long straight section of Plumstead Road. As we motored along, my friend turned his head toward me and asked, "Have you ever traveled at one hundred miles an hour?"

I said, "No."

He responded, "Well, you're about to."

I said, "We don't have to."

He had made up his mind that we would. As he opened the throttle, the motorcycle engine roared, and the machine surged forward. The skin on my face was pulled taut, my shirt billowed and flapped in the wind, and I held on by wrapping my arms tightly around his waist. As he accelerated, I peered fearfully over his shoulder and saw the speedometer needle pass the 98 MPH mark. It was a frightening experience to be placed in a life-threatening situation over which I had no control. But the moment I had accepted the invitation and mounted the passenger seat, I had forfeited my freedom. Fortunately, I survived the harrowing ride, but I determined that day that I would give careful consideration to future invitations before ever entrusting my safety to the control of others.

Many occasions and numerous circumstances in life comparable to my experience with the motorcycle ride are far more dangerous. They may not involve the possibility of physical injury or mortal death, but they have the power to rob us of spiritual well-being and our claim on eternal blessings.

## MAKING DECISIONS

How may we know if it is appropriate to participate in an activity, associate with certain individuals, watch a particular movie or video, attend an event, or immerse ourselves in some kinds of music or literature? Such invitations often seem innocent enough, but our concern ought to be whether these things have the power to contaminate our minds.

We learn from the prophet Nephi to "feast upon the words of Christ; for behold, the words of Christ will tell you all things what ye should do" (2 Nephi 32:3). The scriptures not only provide invaluable insights and education, they also function as a conduit through which we can receive personal inspiration. Consider the words of Moroni: "But behold, that which is of God inviteth and enticeth to do good continually; wherefore, every thing which inviteth and enticeth to do good, and to love God, and to serve him, is inspired of God" (Moroni 7:13).

We possess as a divine heritage a power within that will shield us from deception. Moroni further explains, "For behold, my brethren, it is given unto you to judge, that ye may know good from evil; and the way to judge is as plain, that ye may know with a perfect knowledge, as the daylight is from the dark night. For behold, the Spirit of Christ is given to every man [all the children of God], that he may know good from evil; wherefore, I show unto you the way to judge; for every thing which inviteth to do good, and to persuade to believe in Christ, is sent forth by the power and gift of Christ; wherefore ye may know with a perfect knowledge it is of God" (Moroni 7:15-16).

That this gift is accessible to all who desire and prepare for it is assured in the following verses: "The Spirit [of Christ] giveth light to every man that cometh into the world" (D&C 84:46), and it is through this medium that "men are instructed sufficiently that they [may] know good from evil" (2 Nephi 2:5).

## DRAW NEAR UNTO ME

I later determined that every invitation I accepted and every invitation I extended would be an invitation to come unto Christ—that I would evaluate each activity to ascertain if participation would draw me and others closer to or separate us further from the Savior. Christ's cordial invitation strengthens my resolve to seek his companionship. Consider these words: "And again, verily I say unto you, my friends, I leave these sayings with you to ponder in your hearts, with this commandment which I give unto you, that ye shall call upon me while I am near—Draw near unto me and I will draw near unto you; seek me diligently and ye shall find me; ask, and ye shall receive; knock, and it shall be opened unto you" (D&C 88:62-63). Pondering the possibilities has proven to be an invaluable practice in making important decisions relating to family, Church assignments, and business. I have found that once this pattern is established, the Lord's comforting assurance becomes a reality: "Therefore, you shall feel that it is right" (D&C 9:8).

## HEARKEN UNTO THE COUNSELS OF GOD

A study of human behavior reveals the processes that influence how we act. What we do results from what we think and how we feel about concepts, beliefs, or propositions. The ancient writer of Proverbs understood this: "For [as a man] thinketh in his heart, so is he" (Proverbs 23:7). In a more recent declaration, author James Allen observed: "Whatever your present environment may be, you will fall, remain, or rise with your thoughts, your vision, or your ideals. You will [thus] become as small as your controlling desire, or as great as your dominating aspiration" (*As a Man Thinketh,* 42). It has always been true—how we feel and think dictates the things we do and what we will become. Describing the lamentable state reached by his brothers Laman and Lemuel, Nephi observed that they had become "past feeling" (1 Nephi 17:45) regarding spiritual things.

When we are able to combine our intellect with divine

inspiration, our capacity for discernment and our ability to make wise decisions is magnified beyond our highest expectations. There is danger in depending solely on our own intellect, and the Lord has provided this word of warning: "O that cunning plan of the evil one! O the vainness, and the frailties, and the foolishness of men! When they are learned they think they are wise, and they hearken not unto the counsel of God, for they set it aside, supposing they know of themselves, wherefore, their wisdom is foolishness and it profiteth them not. And they shall perish. But to be learned is good if they hearken unto the counsels of God" (2 Nephi 9:28-29). That is why the Lord encourages us to "seek learning, even by study," but "also by *faith*" (D&C 88:118; emphasis added).

Thus comes the tempering. A quest for, and attainment of, human intellect devoid of the affirmation of the Spirit can leave us isolated from the source of all truth, resulting in a diminished sensitivity to divine direction.

## A MOTHER'S INSPIRATION

The Spirit of Christ, if adhered to, will not only clarify what is right and what is wrong but will warn us of pending danger. An example of this is found in a precious experience I had with my mother.

After my father reported for military service during World War II, my mother was left alone to rear my older brother and me. To her credit, she worked to create for us a secure environment in the midst of insecure circumstances. In those years, Saturday was a special day for our little family, for it was on that day that Mother would take us two boys with her to the city shopping area in Norwich, to a store called Peacock's located in Magdalen Street. We enjoyed our weekly walk together along Telegraph Lane, Bishopsgate, past Saul's Wood Yard, and on to our destination. Part of the excitement on those Saturday outings was the anticipation of the inexpensive treat mother would allow us to purchase from the store. The route taken was always the same, and even the timing of our walk was predictable. As we would pass by the large clock suspended high on the wall by Saul's Wood Yard, its hands would invariably display the time as 10:30 A.M., almost as if fixed in that position. In her endearing Norfolk dialect, Mother would announce with an air of satisfaction, "It's 'aff past ten."

I am sure that my brother was as surprised as I was when one Saturday morning, following our normal preparations, Mother declared, "I don't think we'll go to the shops today." Instead, she suggested that we take a ball to a grassy area in the woodland near our home known as Thorpe Woods. I cannot remember our questioning her suggestion as we happily set out together, and after arriving at the field, my brother and I began kicking the ball to each other. I imagined I was playing in a major soccer tournament in a stadium filled with thousands of cheering spectators. We hadn't been there long when my make-believe thoughts were abruptly interrupted by the distinctive wailing of the air raid siren, and we hastily set off for our home. As we hurried along, we could hear the ominous drone of aircraft engines in the distance.

Arriving at home, we went immediately into the underground air-raid shelter located in the garden at the rear of the house. Huddled together under the shelter's arched, corrugated iron roof, we could hear the sound of exploding bombs close by. (It was not the first time or the last that we would do so. I vividly remember retreating to the shelter one Christmas Eve and wondering if Santa would find us and how he would deliver our gifts with no chimney stack through which to gain entry. I am delighted to report that he left the gifts in our house.) The next day Mother learned that many of the bombs had landed on the area of Saul's Wood Yard, demolishing the buildings, including the large wall clock, and also resulting in loss of life. The bombs had struck the area at 10:30 A.M.! In her later years, my mother repeatedly rehearsed the events of that day, insisting she had been prompted to change her regular routine that morning by what she referred to as a "premonition."

## MANIFESTATIONS OF THE SPIRIT

Even without a full understanding of the source or purpose of this inherent gift, many acknowledge and experience the influence and insights that sometimes come, referring to this phenomenon as "conscience." If we exercise faith and seek confirmation through prayer, the purpose of these promptings, which is to persuade us to believe in Christ, becomes effective in our lives.

The Savior has given us this assurance: "But he that believeth these things which I have spoken, him will I visit with the manifestations of my Spirit, and he shall know and bear record. For because of my Spirit he shall know that these things are true; for it persuadeth men to do good" (Ether 4:11). This verse so aptly describes my own experience in learning to be led by the Spirit and to progress from enjoying *manifestations* of the Holy Spirit to receiving the *companionship* of the Holy Ghost.

## THE GIFT OF THE HOLY GHOST

Following the enticings of the Spirit of Christ leads us through baptism to the gift of the Holy Ghost, of which the scriptures declare, "No man can say that Jesus is the Lord, but by the Holy Ghost" (1 Corinthians 12:3). Matthew 16:13-17 says that while the Savior was at Caesarea Philippi, he asked his disciples, "Whom do men say that I the son of man am?" They replied, "Some say that thou art John the Baptist: some, Elias; and others, Jeremias, or one of the prophets." The question that followed was both personal and penetrating: "He saith unto them, But whom say *ye* that I am? And Simon Peter answered and said, Thou art the Christ, the Son of the living God. And Jesus answered and said unto him, Blessed art thou, Simon Bar-Jona: for flesh and blood hath not revealed it unto thee, but my Father which is in heaven," thus confirming the reality of divine communication through the process of personal revelation.

The value of the gift of the Holy Ghost is inestimable. In the Book of Acts, chapter 8, commencing with verse 9, we read of a certain man called Simon, who had previously bewitched the people of Samaria through the use of sorcery. His deception of the people was particularly devious because his power was thought by the people to have come from God. Philip preached the gospel to those who had been deceived and many, including Simon himself, were baptized. In verses 14 through 17 it says: "Now when the apostles which were at Jerusalem heard that Samaria had received the word of God, they sent unto them Peter and John: Who, when they were come down, prayed for them, that they might receive the Holy Ghost: (For as yet he was fallen upon none of them: only they [had been] baptized in the name of the Lord Jesus.) Then laid they their hands on them, and they received the Holy Ghost."

Witnessing the remarkable effect of this ordinance, Simon offered the apostles money, saying, "Give me also this power, that on whomsoever I lay hands, he may receive the Holy Ghost" (v. 19). Peter responded to his request by saying, "Thy money perish with thee, because thou hast thought that the gift of God may be purchased with money. Thou hast neither part nor lot in this matter: for thy heart is not right in the sight of God" (vv. 20-21).

Following Peter's reprimand, Simon acknowledged the inappropriateness of his request and sought forgiveness. His impulsiveness in making such a proposal was obviously motivated by what he observed and the impression it had on him. The prophet of the Restoration, Joseph Smith, described the dramatic result of having the Holy Ghost fall on him and Oliver Cowdery: "Our minds being now enlightened, we began to have the scriptures laid open to our understandings, and the true meaning and intention of their more mysterious passages revealed unto us in a manner which we never could attain to previously, nor ever before had thought of" (JS-H 1:74).

## THE COMPANIONSHIP OF THE HOLY GHOST

These accounts convey the supernal nature and origin of this extraordinary gift described in John 15:26 as "the Spirit of truth." For those who recognize the purpose and value of the Holy Ghost, the quest for its constant companionship is never ending. The Savior's disciples in the land of Bountiful among the people of Nephi expressed their feelings in these words: "And they did pray for that which they most desired; and they desired that the Holy Ghost should be given unto them" (3 Nephi 19:9). It is apparent that they desired this gift more than any other.

In this same chapter the Savior expressed his gratitude to the Father in the following manner: "Father, I thank thee that thou hast given the Holy Ghost unto these whom I have chosen; and it is because of their belief in me that I have chosen them out of the world. Father, I pray thee that thou wilt give the Holy Ghost unto all them that shall believe in their words" (vv. 20-21).

I can confirm that this promise is fulfilled as our faith increases and as we attune our lives to the Master's message. Then we discover a tranquillity that would otherwise elude us.

We are not left without guidance. If we will nurture the feelings that come as a result of the promptings of the Spirit, we will develop a remarkable capacity to make decisions that will be of eternal benefit, and "our joy shall be full forever" (2 Nephi 9:18).

# THE UNRIPE APPLES

## THE INTRUDERS

Another childhood experience comes to mind.

Close to the home where I was reared as a child was what appeared to me to be a very large house. It was located on beautiful grounds surrounded by a fence made of wood paneling rising to the height of six feet. I recall peeping through knotholes in the panels. It was like looking through a telescope capable of exploring another world. The beautifully manicured lawns, the well-kept flower gardens, and a small orchard provided an idyllic setting for the brick and decorative stone exterior of the house. Unfortunately, the opportunity to enjoy the view was always brief due to a vigilant British bulldog that patrolled the gardens and that was immediately attracted to anyone standing close to the exterior of the fencing. Even though the fierce dog was confined in the garden, the sound of his sniffing was enough to make me run away from the fence and out of danger of being mauled. A pair of schoolteachers, Mr. and Mrs. Lyons, lived in the home. To add to the intrigue, Mr. Lyons had no right hand, using instead a steel hook that protruded below the cuff of his jacket. In my boyish mind, I often imagined Mr. Lyons pursuing me and catching me by the collar with that hook.

I recall an August morning when I was ten or eleven years old. Following a night of unusually strong winds, I was greeted by friends as I left my home. They were obviously excited and inquired, "Did you hear the wind last night?"

When I said I had, they proceeded to tell me what they had discovered: the wind had blown down sections of the fencing surrounding the Lyons's home.

I couldn't understand why this would cause so much excitement and asked them to explain the significance. They responded with even greater enthusiasm.

"We have access to the apple trees!"

I was still very cautious and asked, "But what about Mr. Lyons?"

"Mr. and Mrs. Lyons are not at home; they are away visiting relatives."

"Where is the dog?" I probed.

"Locked in the kennel," came the reply.

My friends had certainly carried out detailed research, and we headed for our target with all haste. Entering the yard, we climbed the trees and hastily plucked the fruit, filling our pockets and also the space between our shirts and our bodies. The flow of adrenaline was high since I feared that any moment the dog or Mr. Lyons, or both, would appear in the garden and apprehend us. We ran from the scene of our trespass to a secluded place in a nearby wooded area, and after regaining our composure began to consume the apples.

It was August, and the apples were not yet ripe enough to be sweet. However, the tartness of the green apples did not deter us as we enthusiastically consumed our spoils, acting out of a compulsion I cannot now explain. After devouring a significant number, I contented myself with taking a bite out of each remaining apple and throwing the remnants of the fruit into the nearby bushes.

## SUFFERING THE CONSEQUENCES

The frivolity diminished as our bodies began to gradually react to the invasion they had experienced. The chemical reaction between my gastric juices and the unripe apples caused me to experience stomach cramps and to feel nauseated.

As I sat regretting what I had done, I realized that a feeling within me was producing even more discomfort than the unripe apples. It was the realization that what I had done was wrong. When my friends had proposed that we invade the garden, I had felt uncomfortable but lacked the courage to say no and so suppressed my feelings. Now, after the deed had been accomplished, I was filled with remorse. To my regret, I had ignored the prompting that our adventure was wrong. Just as the radar beam safely guides a jet airliner to its destination, so the light within, if we respond to it, will guide us through the dark and foggy days of life along the course that will lead us safely home.

## SELF-RESTRAINT

There is not a wall thick enough or a fence high enough to keep us from pursuing deviant paths if we are determined to do so. But there is a still, small voice within each of us that, when recognized and responded to, will keep us from succumbing to temptation. My experience with the apples was not in vain, as it awakened my sensitivity to the value of this inherent compass.

Several weeks later I joined my friends in the wooded area previously mentioned, anticipating that we would devise some activity or game to play. As I approached them, they were huddled together. I saw smoke rising in the air above them and recognized the aroma of burning tobacco. One of them had obtained a packet of cigarettes, and they were smoking. They invited me to join them, and when I declined, they ridiculed and taunted me with condescending remarks. But nothing they could say or do persuaded me to change my mind. I had not been reared with a knowledge of the restored gospel and the Word of Wisdom, but I knew by a feeling within that I should not participate with them.

As I walked home, reflecting on the action I had taken, I felt good inside. Although my expectations for the day had not materialized and I would have to find a way to occupy my time without my friends, I had discovered something about myself—about the source of real happiness and the invigoration that results from making the right decision, whatever the circumstances.

## SAFEGUARDING SACRED SENSITIVITY

We learn from the scriptures that if we persistently override or ignore this divinely implanted warning system, it can become dulled and inoperative. Exposure to degrading materials, participation in or association with unseemly activities, or violent behavior can desensitize us, creating the conditions described by Mormon in the second epistle to his son Moroni: "And now, my son, I dwell no longer upon this horrible scene. Behold, thou knowest the wickedness of this people; thou knowest that they are without principle, and past feeling" (Moroni 9:20).

Witnessing violence, deceit, or unfaithfulness in a real-life situation or as a fictional representation causes me extreme discomfort. Fortunately, my encounters with actual incidents have been minimal, and by exercising my capacity to choose, I have been able to shield my mind from what to me would have been unpleasant, unnecessary, and unwelcome intrusions.

So many voices compete for our attention that we can be overwhelmed. The scriptures express this thought in these words: "There are, it may be, so many kinds of voices in the world, and none of them is without signification"

(1 Corinthians 14:10). Amidst the crescendo of sound comes the divine invitation to "be still and know that I am God" (D&C 101:16). As we take the time to ponder and as we develop the ability to listen, we can study things out in our minds and discern that which is right.

## HARNESSING HEAVENLY SUPPORT

This approach does not restrict our pursuit of truth and reason; in fact, the opposite occurs. As we identify and harness this dimension of our being, our horizons enlarge and our vision of possibilities expands.

The danger lies in the universal tendency described in the scriptures: "Every way of a man is right in his own eyes" (Proverbs 21:2).

If we become predominately self-opinioned and introverted, we miss the wider expanse of available knowledge. Though this warning is aimed at priesthood holders, it applies to all of us: "When we undertake to cover our sins, or to gratify our pride, our vain ambition, or to exercise control or dominion or compulsion upon the souls of the children of men, in any degree of unrighteousness, behold, the heavens *withdraw themselves;* the Spirit of the Lord is grieved; and *when it is withdrawn,* Amen to the priesthood or the authority of that man. Behold, ere he is aware, *he is left unto himself*" (D&C 121:37-38; emphasis added). That is, we are left to the limitations of our own wisdom and ability. In the great vision he was given of the scope of God's creations, Moses discovered the spiritual loneliness that is created when the Spirit of the Lord withdraws from man. "And the presence of God withdrew from Moses, that his glory was not upon Moses; and Moses *was left unto himself*" (Moses 1:9; emphasis added). Moses thereby discovered the dramatic difference between the power and glory of Deity and the relatively meager capacities of mankind. From the book of Job we also learn that "there is a spirit in man: and the inspiration of the Almighty giveth [him] understanding" (Job 32:8).

We consist of more than the physical frame and temporal being that is visibly discernible. We are spirit children of God clothed in mortal bodies. During our formative mortal years, our spirit is attuned to the Spirit of Christ in a way similar to the way a radio receiver is attuned to radio waves. However, if we persistently ignore this source of enlightenment, we can dull our ability to discern its prompting. The Lord has in fact cautioned us that his "Spirit will not always strive with man" (Ether 2:15). As we mature we experience an increasing tendency to become more self-sufficient and resistant to things that cannot be readily explained or clearly defined. Too many of us discount the existence of a divine creator, choosing to rely in our mortal journey more on the philosophies and theories of man than on the promptings of the Holy Ghost or the teachings found in the scriptures. Alma's encounter with Korihor, related in Chapter 30 of Alma in the Book of Mormon, captures the classic conflict that can ensue.

## INCONTROVERTIBLE EVIDENCE

Following Korihor's declaration that there is no God, Alma poses the question, "And now what evidence have ye that there is no God, or that Christ cometh not? I say unto you that ye have none, save it be your word only. But, behold, I have all things as a testimony that these things are true; and ye also have all things as a testimony unto you that they are true; and will ye deny them? Believest thou that these things are true?" (vv. 40–41).

In response, Korihor issues a challenge to Alma: "If thou wilt show me a sign, that I may be convinced that there is a God, . . . then will I be convinced of the truth of thy words" (v. 43). Knowing that signs are ineffective in such a debate, Alma responds: "Thou hast had signs enough; will ye tempt your God? Will ye say, Show unto me a sign, when ye have the testimony of all these thy brethren, and also all the holy prophets? The scriptures are laid before thee, yea, and all things denote there is a God; yea, even the earth, and all things that are upon the face of it, yea, and its motion, yea, and also all the planets which move in their regular form do witness that there is a Supreme Creator" (v. 44).

My faith is secure regarding the existence and character of God. I am indeed "compassed about with so great a cloud of witnesses" (Hebrews 12:1). By comparison, all other options are devoid of power and purpose, and they diminish the dignity of mankind. All of creation declares and provides evidence of the verity of God. That which can be seen is a witness of that which is hidden from the natural eye. A latter-day revelation makes reference to the earth, the sun, and the moon, followed by this insightful statement: "Any man who hath seen any or the least of these hath seen God moving in his majesty and power" (D&C 88:47).

## CONVICTION AND COORDINATES

My personal testimony and ever-growing faith had their beginnings in seemingly insignificant everyday events. Reflections on intimations of the Spirit, initially barely discernible, eventually became so prominent that they were impossible for me to ignore.

Each of these experiences—the motorcycle ride, Mother's inspiration, the stolen apples, and the invitation to smoke a cigarette—taught me invaluable lessons and awakened my sensitivity to what many refer to as an inborn instinct but which I have come to recognize as the Spirit of Christ.

Ancient mariners and travelers discovered the necessity of charting their course by focusing on things that were constant and unchanging. They used the stars and landmarks that provided reliable indicators that would ensure a safe journey to their desired destination. The sextant and compass were navigational instruments designed to more accurately determine location. Technological developments have resulted in the computerized navigational systems of our day.

Considering the complex, sophisticated systems now in use, I was surprised to read an interesting fact in an October 1992 newspaper article reporting the open house activities prior to the rededication of the London Temple. Commercial airline pilots operating out of London's Gatwick Airport were, it was reported, delighted to learn that the temple would be operational again. It seems they had been using the temple's lighted spire as a landmark in their approach to the airport runway.

Yes, man has always depended on course markers, whether heavenly constellations or earthly landmarks, to get his bearings. There is a more important journey on which all have embarked. That is the journey of life for which there is also a purpose and a plan. The following words expressed by a loving father to his son provide enlightening insights into how we can plot our course in the most important journey of all: "For behold, it is as easy to give heed to the word of Christ, which will point to you a straight course to eternal bliss, as it was for our fathers to give heed to this compass [the Liahona], which would point unto them a straight course to the promised land.

"And now I say, is there not a type in this thing? For just as surely as this director did bring our fathers, by following its course, to the promised land, shall the words of Christ, if we follow their course, carry us beyond this vale of sorrow into a far better land of promise.

"O my son, do not let us be slothful because of the easiness of the way; for so was it with our fathers; for so was it prepared for them, that if they would look they might live; even so it is with us. The way is prepared, and if we will look we may live forever.

"And now, my son, see that ye take care of these sacred things, yea, see that ye look to God and live " (Alma 37:44–47).

## THE PLAN PLOTS A SURE COURSE

Brigham Young observed, "You cannot find a compass on the earth, that points, so directly, as the Gospel plan of salvation. It has a place for every thing, and puts everything in its place" (*Journal of Discourses*, 3:96).

With a knowledge of the Lord's plan of salvation and the guidance of the Spirit, we can chart a course in life that will allow us not only to enjoy our mortal journey but also to arrive at our divinely appointed destination.

Becoming aware of and responding to this source of divine direction is, I am convinced, essential to attaining an understanding of the Lord's plan that will lead all that follow to rejoice as they "draw water out of the wells of salvation" (2 Nephi 22:3).

It is my belief that this precious gift is available to all who desire it and who learn to be led by the Spirit.

# "CAN YOU HEAR
# THE CLICKING SOUND?"

### DISTINCTIVE AND UNMISTAKABLE

I was thrilled one day during my printing apprenticeship when the plant supervisor advised me that he had decided to put me in charge of a press. This was, he declared, an expression of confidence in my developing ability. The machine to which I was assigned applied a glossy coating to preprinted food product labels in a complicated process that transferred a gloss solution from an ink duct, via rollers, to a metal surface that moved under a rotating cylinder carrying sheets of paper on which the labels had been previously printed. My responsibility was to set up the machine and to hand-feed individual sheets into it.

Oliver and Colin, both qualified machine minders, conducted my training. When the time came for me to assume responsibility, they gave me some final words of instruction. They were the words of experienced tradesmen to a novice, indicating that to properly operate my machine, I would have to learn to listen for a certain "clicking" noise.

"Can you hear that clicking sound?" Colin asked.

I listened to the cacophony of sound coming from the

machine. Metal gears were meshing, grippers were opening and closing, and hundreds of other coordinated mechanical functions were going on simultaneously. All of that produced an undecipherable clatter.

I listened for a moment and, hearing a sound that I felt matched his description, responded affirmatively. He reemphasized the importance of listening for the clicking sound, repeating that it was an indicator that the machine was functioning properly.

This was the moment I had waited for; I was manning the machine without supervision. Everything went well for approximately forty-five minutes. Then my sense of well-being was shattered by a loud bang! I pushed the stop button, and the machine shuddered to a halt.

Having heard the loud noise, my fellow workers gathered from around the workshop, interested to discover what had caused the commotion. As I stepped down from the wooden platform to inspect my press, I could see pieces of paper wrapped around the rollers and compressed in the gear mechanism.

My trainer arrived on the scene and inquired what had happened. I said that I did not know. He helped me remove the debris from the machine rollers and mechanism, added thinners to the gloss in the ink duct, and reset the press. Within minutes, he had the machine purring again as if nothing had happened. Before leaving the machine to my care, he repeated his previous instructions, once again asking, "Can you hear that clicking sound?"

I listened until I heard what I thought he was describing and said yes. With my self-esteem dented by this traumatic experience, I cautiously proceeded to feed sheets of paper into the machine. Forty to forty-five minutes later, just as I was regaining my confidence, the machine once again jammed.

This time Colin said that I would have to clean up the press without his assistance. My unfortunate circumstances were viewed with great hilarity by work colleagues as they watched me self-consciously complete this difficult task. When the cleanup was completed, Colin repeated the set-up procedures and again set the machine in motion. As we stood side-by-side on the machine platform, he asked me for the third time, "Can you hear that clicking sound?"

I listened intently. The air was filled with the sound of revolving rollers, whirring gears, and many other mechanical sounds. But suddenly I detected a new sound, clearly and distinctively distinguishable from all the other sounds. It could best be described as a sort of "clicking sound." It was caused by the sheets of paper passing over a metal plate. When the consistency of the gloss was right, the clicking sound to which Colin had referred was generated at the moment the paper separated from the metal. Having learned what to listen for, I felt confident I could keep the press working properly.

It can be difficult to discern the voice of the Spirit, but like the clicking sound, once discovered, it is distinctive and unmistakable.

## THE DIVINE DIMENSION

As we strive to learn gospel principles, we restrict our understanding if we conclude that the full message is expressed in the words that are spoken. I have been impressed on many occasions by the realization that when the prophets speak, they feel and know more than I hear. Since my call as a General Authority, I have discovered that though I may teach the same things and use the same vocabulary as I did before my call, what I *feel* while doing so has changed significantly. That is why, unless we too are familiar with the voice of the Spirit, it is extremely difficult to fully identify with others when they speak of spiritual experiences. Because it is easy for us to be misunderstood, the Lord has also cautioned us about sharing in public settings what are intended to be personal revelations—unless the Spirit prompts us to do so.

My experiences with the Spirit of Christ before my conversion provided a wonderful preparation for when, following my baptism and my confirmation, I was promised, if worthy, that I would enjoy the companionship of the Holy Ghost. I gradually developed a sensitivity to this sacred gift that has brought the blessing of discernment and a greater dimension of wisdom. I have also noticed that, as spiritually enriching as my ministry has been, I have received no greater guidance than in the area of my role as a husband and father.

## THE VOICE OF THE SPIRIT

An example of the workings of the Spirit is found in the following experience.

An elderly sister who had been cared for by my wife, Pamela, expressed her appreciation by giving Pamela a ring that had been a family heirloom. The woman had no other surviving members in her family, and she wanted Pamela to be the beneficiary. By our standard, it was a very valuable ring, but its real value was in the friendship it represented and the love and gratitude it conveyed.

Pamela didn't often wear the ring but treated it with great care. On one occasion when Pamela was wearing the ring, one of the claws securing its precious stone snagged on her clothing. Fearing the stone might fall out of its setting, my wife removed it from her finger, wrapped it in a facial tissue, and put it for temporary safekeeping in her makeup bag. When she looked for the ring several days later, she could not find it. Pamela concluded that the ring had likely been discarded into the refuse with the tissue. By the time she discovered the loss, the refuse collectors had already visited our home and cleared the refuse bin, emptying its contents into their vehicle and hauling it away. Pamela was distressed by what had happened and the manner in which the gift had been lost. I expressed sympathy without giving the matter deep consideration.

Two days later, I startled Pamela by abruptly sitting up in bed after awaking from the night's sleep. Responding to an impression I had felt, I added to her surprise by saying, "The ring is in the refuse bin!" Believing I was dreaming, Pamela responded, "It may have been in the bin, but the bin has been emptied, so the ring would no longer be there." I repeated my statement with assurance and conviction.

Dressed in clothing I kept for home work projects, and slipping my hands into a pair of rubber gloves, I headed for the refuse bin to conduct another search.

Refuse from the previous two days had already been deposited. I lifted this out onto a plastic sheet and sorted through it, uncovering among other things straw and debris from the hutch that housed two guinea pigs we kept as family pets. Sifting through the straw, I located a crumpled piece of tissue paper. Nestled in the paper was the missing ring. Pamela was amazed when I came back into the house and handed the ring to her.

I don't wish to imply that in every circumstance the outcome has been so favorable or the result so dramatic, but I have clearly discerned the voice of the Spirit on numerous occasions, particularly when it was necessary to respond to the needs of others or to know the will of the Lord. This has been especially evident when I have been assigned to determine who the Lord has prepared to serve as the president of a stake during the reorganization of a stake presidency.

The voice of the Spirit most often manifests itself as a feeling, and through such feelings, the Holy Ghost can teach us the truth of all things. The Lord has counseled us to "put [our] trust in that Spirit which leadeth to good—yea, to do justly, to walk humbly, to judge righteously; and this is my Spirit. Verily, verily, I say unto you, I will impart unto you of my Spirit, which shall enlighten your mind, which shall fill your soul with joy" (D&C 11:12–13).

## I WILL POUR OUT MY SPIRIT

An assignment to Iceland provided an opportunity for me to gain a broader comprehension of how the Spirit operates in teaching and learning the gospel.

It was Sunday morning, and the Saints were assembling in a small chapel in Reykjavik for a district conference. As we watched from the stand as the people took their seats, the mission president commented that these were remarkable people. I knew that they were but asked him to qualify his statement. He reminded me that there were few roads crossing the island and that to attend the meeting, many of the people had traveled on the perimeter highway, a roundabout journey that for some had taken six to eight hours. As we sat waiting for the meeting to commence, I pondered what the president had said. Faithful Saints had gathered at some inconvenience to be instructed and edified. What could I say in my address that would justify the time they had spent traveling and the sacrifices they had made?

When it was my turn to speak, I stood at the pulpit praying that the Lord would bless me with a message commensurate to their faith. With an interpreter at my side, I had more time than usual to consider my words, and I thoughtfully structured every sentence. After concluding with my testimony, I returned to my seat, hoping that my words had been worthy of such dedicated Saints.

Following the singing of a hymn and a benediction on the meeting, I stepped down from the stand and saw in the faces of many of the Saints expressions of appreciation, and I received other indications that they had enjoyed an enriching experience. It was then that the light of understanding distilled upon me. Their experience had little to do with my ability to teach. They had been taught by the Spirit in response to their faith. I have never forgotten that experience or the lesson learned. Touching hearts and creating a desire to change results not from an eloquence of speech or demonstration of intellect. When learning takes place, it is a gift of the Spirit to those who have prepared themselves to receive it. "Therefore, why is it that ye cannot understand and know, that he that receiveth the word by the Spirit of truth receiveth it as it is preached by the Spirit of truth? Wherefore, he that preacheth and he that receiveth, understand one another, and both are edified and rejoice together" (D&C 50:21–22).

I have often marveled at how differently members of the same congregation can respond to the same meeting. One person will proclaim it a spiritual feast while another will declare it a waste of time. Such diversity of opinion can be traced in part to the difference in the degree of faith and interest that participants bring to the meeting. Such was apparently true, even in the primitive Church. Paul wrote: "For unto us was the gospel preached, as well as unto them: but the word preached did not profit them, not being mixed with faith in them that heard it" (Hebrews 4:2).

## THE PROMISE

We are promised that if we will prepare ourselves, we "shall be taught from on high" (D&C 43:16). What a glorious possibility! Instead of being limited to receiving instruction, acquiring information, or gaining knowledge from fellow beings, we have access to a pure source of truth that enables us to drink from the fountainhead instead of a murky estuary. It is true that the Lord reveals his word to his servants the prophets in matters relating to the Church and mankind in general, but he will also guide us individually in our responsibilities as fathers and mothers, in our Church assignments, and in the conduct of our lives. In John 14:15-17, we read how this principle operates: "If ye love me, keep my commandments. And I will pray the Father, and he shall give you another Comforter, that he may abide with you for ever; Even the Spirit of truth; whom the world cannot receive." It is apparent from other scriptural passages that reference to *the world* refers to the disobedient, the unrepentant, and those who reject the enticings of the Spirit. For instance, in Joseph Smith's translation of Matthew we find this enlightening definition: "The destruction of the wicked, which is the end of the world" (JS-M 1:4).

In promising his disciples the gift of the Holy Ghost, the Savior explained that only those who are spiritually attuned are able to receive the Holy Spirit's prompting. He who is of "the world" (whose view is restricted to the temporal plain) cannot receive the Comforter "because it seeth him not, neither knoweth him." But because they were faithful, the disciples were told: "But ye know him; for he dwelleth with you, and shall be in you" (John 14:17).

Further describing the benefits and qualities associated with the receipt of this divine gift, the Lord explained, "But the Comforter, which is the Holy Ghost, whom the Father will send in my name, he shall teach you all things, and bring all things to your remembrance, whatsoever I have said unto you" (John 14:26). This promise is made to everyone who becomes a disciple of Christ by following the pattern and path established by the mortal Messiah. He came unto John the Baptist to be baptized of him even though he himself was guilty of no sin, thus marking the course we must all follow. "And Jesus, when he was baptized, went up straightway out of the water: and, lo, the heavens were opened unto him, and he saw the Spirit of God descending like a dove, and lighting upon him" (Matthew 3:16). Having been tutored and authorized by the

Master, Peter and John and the other apostles continued the practice of bestowing the gift of the Holy Ghost on those who joined the early Christian Church (see Acts 8:12–17).

## HAVE YE RECEIVED THE HOLY GHOST?

The New Testament account of Apollos and his experience is of particular interest to me. We read that Apollos was "an eloquent man, and mighty in the scriptures." He taught from the words of the Old Testament prophets that were available to him. We learn more of his capacity in the next verse wherein it states, "This man was instructed in the way of the Lord; and being fervent in the spirit, he spake and taught diligently the things of the Lord, knowing only the baptism of John" (Acts 18:24–25).

Apollos was a powerful teacher: "For he mightily convinced the Jews, and that publickly, shewing by the scriptures that Jesus was Christ" (Acts 18:28). Based on his success, one might conclude that Apollos was fully empowered to teach the gospel and administer its ordinances. But when Paul met certain disciples of Christ who had apparently been taught the gospel and perhaps been baptized by Apollos, he found it necessary to put things in order.

"Have ye received the Holy Ghost since ye believed?" he inquired of them. They responded, "We have not so much as heard whether there be any Holy Ghost." Perceiving by this that their baptisms were not valid, Paul directed that they be baptized properly by one having legitimate authority to perform the ordinance. Then, "when Paul had laid his hands upon them, the Holy Ghost came on them" (Acts 19:2, 6).

This episode demonstrates the necessity of being baptized by one authorized to act in the name of God. It also clarifies that the gift of the Holy Ghost is bestowed by the laying on of hands by one having authority to perform the ordinance.

It is therefore not surprising to find this ordinance practiced in The Church of Jesus Christ of Latter-day Saints in our day. The Prophet Joseph Smith declared, "The ordinances of the Gospel were laid out before the foundations of the world" (*Teachings of the Prophet Joseph Smith*, 367). They cannot be changed or altered; all must be saved on the same principles.

## WHAT GREATER WITNESS

Paul testified that he derived his understanding of the gospel from a divine source. "But I certify you, brethren, that the gospel which was preached of me is not after man. For I neither received it of man, neither was I taught it, but by the revelation of Jesus Christ" (Galatians 1:11-12).

Oliver Cowdery had an experience that suggests how the Spirit of the Lord blesses us. Oliver had been seeking a witness of the truth of Joseph Smith's testimony, and the Lord said to Oliver: "Verily, verily, I say unto you, if you desire a further witness, cast your mind upon the night that you cried unto me in your heart, that you might know concerning the truth of these things. Did I not speak peace to your mind concerning the matter? What greater witness can you have than from God?" (D&C 6:22-23).

I can think of no better way to describe my own witness and the confidence that I feel. The Lord has indeed spoken *peace to my mind* concerning divine truths that can be discerned only through revelation. Paul wrote: "The things of God knoweth no man, but the Spirit of God. Now we have received, not the spirit of the world, but the spirit which is of God; that we might know the things that are freely given to us of God. Which things also we speak, not in the words which man's wisdom teacheth, but which the Holy Ghost teacheth; comparing spiritual things with spiritual. But the natural man receiveth not the things of the Spirit of God: for they are foolishness unto him: neither can he know them, because they are spiritually discerned" (1 Corinthians 2:11-14).

The "clicking sound" referred to earlier is a simple example, but it reminds me that in order to "hear" the word of the Lord, we must learn to identify his voice. I can declare with the utmost assurance, born of a personal witness, that if we prepare ourselves, exercise faith as disciples of Christ, and remain worthy, we can receive the promptings of the Holy Ghost and thereby feel what is right and be filled with joy.

# HE SHALL MAKE THINGS KNOWN UNTO US

## ARE WE HEADING IN THE RIGHT DIRECTION?

Great experiences in life often result when current events and celebrations are garnished by recollections from the past. The memory of moments shared with those we love can be awakened by what we see, hear, and feel. When we are separated from our family and friends during traditional gatherings such as Christmas, we often reminisce about memorable events and reflect on their significance.

In 1969 I had just such an experience, one that has since served to remind me of an important principle. It was Christmas Eve, and Pamela and I had driven twenty-eight miles to visit members of our extended family. We had enjoyed a wonderful evening, traveling from house to house, exchanging gifts, sharing news, and expressing our love for one another. Returning to the car after making the last delivery, our thoughts turned to home. Kevin, our three-year-old son, had not been feeling well, and Pamela's younger sister, Susan, had stayed at our home to take care of him. Thinking of Kevin, I was filled with an overwhelming desire to be reunited as a

family on that special night when we of a Christian faith cele-
brate the Savior's birth.

As we began our journey home, I decided to take an alter-
nate route, which I thought would shorten our travel time.
Without consulting a map or discussing my intentions with
Pamela, I looked for the earliest opportunity to leave the
known road to find a better way. After some distance, the beam
of the car headlights finally illuminated a road junction ahead
of us. Filled with assurance that I knew what I was doing, I
turned off the main road into what was a very narrow lane.

When Pamela asked, "Are we heading in the right direction?" I assured her that we were. But the farther we traveled,
the narrower the lane became.

Pamela asked again, "Are you sure?"

I responded with confidence, "Yes! Of course I am."

Almost as soon as I spoke these words, we passed between
a set of gateposts and drove into a freshly plowed field. Pamela
said nothing as I struggled to maneuver the vehicle out of the
mud, over the slippery surface, back between the gateposts,
and onto the country lane I had chosen to follow.

I must confess that I realized I had made a wrong decision
as soon as we left the known road, but I said nothing. After
extricating the car from the plowed field, we returned in
silence to the junction with the main highway. I was in a contemplative mood and was not comforted when we noticed a
road sign pointing in the direction of our ill-fated detour:
"Unsuitable for Motor Vehicles." It wasn't until years later that
I came across Elder Boyd K. Packer's pertinent statement: "We
cannot set off on a wrong course without first overruling a
warning." That was a bit of counsel I might have used earlier.

We continued our journey home by the known way, taking more time than was necessary because of my desire to find
a shortcut. Reflecting upon our experience, I regretted not

having consulted a map, not stopping to read the road sign, not discussing my intentions with Pamela, and not responding to the feeling within that prompted me immediately as I turned off the highway that I had not made a good decision.

We have often laughed since about my insistence that I knew what I was doing, even as we came to a stop in that plowed field. And as Christmas approaches each year, I am reminded of Pamela's question: "Are we heading in the right direction?" The experience has served as a wonderful reminder to me to periodically reconsider my relationship with the Savior. Do I feel nearer to him, and have I become more like him than a year ago? That is a question we all might well ask ourselves.

## THE EVENTS SURROUNDING CHRISTMAS

We all look forward to Christmas, but do we really comprehend the significance of our celebration? I recall another family experience that helped me gain a greater appreciation for this special holiday.

The first year our son, Kevin, was old enough to begin enjoying Christmas, Pamela and I were very excited. We both had fond memories of our own childhood experiences, and we were eager to provide similar memories for him. On Christmas morning, with the three of us seated together on the floor of our home near the Christmas tree, we began distributing the gifts. Kevin was immediately attracted by the colorful wrapping paper and was enjoying playing with the packages. Eventually Pamela loosened the wrapping paper on one, anticipating that Kevin would then discover the gift concealed within. He continued to find the paper more interesting and attractive than the present. It was only when he tired of playing with the wrapping that he finally discovered the gift inside.

As I observed the events of that Christmas morning, I pondered my own appreciation for the real gift wrapped in traditional Christmas festivities. Like children, we can easily be distracted from the real reason for rejoicing by the trappings of our celebration.

The joy of which the angels sang at the time of Christ's mortal birth is not found in the dazzling array of decorations or even in the exchanging of carefully chosen gifts. It is not even found in the superficial singing of carols. It can be discovered only by extending ourselves in service to others and through accepting the invitation to "draw near unto me and I will draw near unto you; seek me diligently and ye shall find me" (D&C 88:63).

## TWO BOYS AND A BATTLESHIP

An event from my own childhood illustrates how tragically unaware of circumstances we can become if our selfish expectations become the central focus of our lives. It was 1945, and my brother and I were looking forward to Christmas with great anticipation. Our father was serving overseas in the British Army, and Mother was struggling to provide for us in the face of food rationing and other limited resources. Because she had worked so hard to shield us from the reality of those dark and difficult days, my brother and I were blissfully ignorant of what must have been her many concerns.

As is the custom with most children, Clive and I awakened early Christmas morning, delighted to discover that the empty pillow cases we had placed at the foot of our bed the night before were filled with parcels. We rummaged through the packages, unwrapping them to discover fruit, nuts, and articles of clothing—essential items—but no clockwork cars, gadgets or games, picture books, or model planes. I was disappointed and expressed my feelings. Whenever I revisit that scene in my mind, I feel ashamed of myself and my reprehensible reaction. I cannot imagine how badly my mother must have felt as she observed my behavior.

That year my Uncle Alfred and Aunt Maud spent Christmas at my grandparents' home, which adjoined our home. A wooden fence approximately five feet high separated the backyards of our two homes. It was not unusual for a head to appear above the fencing, accompanied by the call of my grandfather or grandmother to attract attention when they had a message to convey or needed someone to run an errand for them.

Later that particular Christmas morning, we heard a voice calling and looked from our living room window to see Uncle Alfred looking over the fence. He beckoned us to come to him. As Clive and I did so, Uncle Alfred said, "Father Christmas must have been confused; he left a present for you with us." Then he handed us a model of a battleship made from matchboxes. From a hole in the side of the vessel trailed a piece of string, which, when tugged sharply, would release the mechanism of a mouse trap located in the hold of the ship and throw matchboxes in all directions.

Clive and I were delighted with the homemade toy. Over and over we reassembled the battleship, then played an imaginary game, which culminated in the demolition of the ship. That matchbox ship remains one of the most memorable Christmas gifts of my childhood. It turned an ungrateful boy into one that was overflowing with gratitude. However, the value of the gift was not in its cost but in the creativity and thoughtfulness of the giver. I will never forget the joy that radiated from the eyes and face of Uncle Alfred as he watched us enjoy playing with the gift he had so cleverly constructed.

In his writings to early Church members, the Apostle Paul expressed feelings similar to those I associate with that Christmas: "So being affectionately desirous of you, we were willing to have imparted unto you, not the gospel of God only, but also our own souls, because ye were dear unto us" (1 Thessalonians 2:8).

## OUR SAVIOR'S BIRTH

I learned from that long-ago experience that the greatest gift is the giving of oneself for the benefit of others—something perfectly exemplified in the birth, life, and atoning sacrifice of the Savior of the world.

I enjoy thinking of the events associated with his birth and of those chosen few who were invited to witness for themselves the humble circumstances that greeted his arrival as a babe in Bethlehem. Imagine the joy experienced by the shepherds who were blessed to hear the angel declare, "Fear not: for, behold, I bring you good tidings of great joy" and who were also told that this message was "to all people." They were invited to be present at what is one of the most significant events in the history of mankind. The angel continued with the words, "For unto you is born this day in the city of David a Saviour, which is Christ the Lord. And this shall be a sign unto you; Ye shall find the babe wrapped in swaddling clothes, lying in a manger." A previously unseen throng of heavenly beings who had observed this sacred moment could no longer restrain themselves. The scriptures record, "And suddenly there was with the angel a multitude of the heavenly host praising God, and saying, Glory to God in the highest, and on earth peace, good will toward men." The shepherds then said to one another, "Let us now go even unto Bethlehem, and see this thing which is come to pass, which the Lord hath made known unto us" (Luke 2:10–15).

We may not see an angel or hear a heavenly choir, but the voice of the Spirit can enlighten our minds and touch our hearts so that we can recognize the truth. The impact of the heavenly host on the shepherds was evident in their response.

"And they came with haste, and found Mary, and Joseph, and the babe lying in a manger" (Luke 2:16).

Do we respond in a similar manner to the invitation to find the Lord? Are we heading in the right direction? Simeon, an old man who is described as "just and devout," had been led by the Spirit into the temple, and "when the parents brought in the child Jesus . . . then took he him up in his arms, and blessed God, and said, Lord, now lettest thou thy servant depart in peace, according to thy word: For mine eyes have seen thy salvation" (Luke 2:25-30). The child's identity was made known unto Simeon by the Lord through the Holy Ghost. In like manner, the Lord can make things known unto us.

The wise men who were led by the light of a star arrived later, for we read, "And when they were come into the house, they saw the young child with Mary his mother, and fell down, and worshiped him" (Matthew 2:11). All who traveled to see the Christ child did so because of a divine influence. The scriptures teach, "And every one that hearkeneth to the voice of the Spirit cometh unto God" (D&C 84:47). This is the process by which sacred things are made known unto us. The Spirit is the compass within, which, if followed, will guide us safely home to the Lord's presence.

## FINDING OUR WAY

Another family experience I had while traveling reminds me of the difficulties often associated with finding the right way. We had driven by car to an unfamiliar community to visit a friend who was recuperating in the hospital following an illness. As we approached an intersection where several roads converged, I was relieved to see a road sign marked with the word "Hospital," indicating the direction we should go. With this reassurance, we continued our journey. But after searching for some time without finding a hospital, we concluded we had gone the wrong way. We decided to return to the intersection to check the sign once more. As we approached, we noticed that the signpost was not secure and had been free to move with every gust of wind to a different position, providing an unreliable point of reference. Stopping to ask directions, we finally reached our destination.

How can we be sure that we are traveling in the right direction? To guide us in life's journey, the Savior has given this promise to his faithful followers: "If ye love me, keep my commandments. And I will pray the Father, and he shall give you another Comforter, that he may abide with you for ever; Even the Spirit of truth; whom the world cannot receive, because it seeth him not, neither knoweth him: but ye know him; for he dwelleth with you, and shall be in you" (John 14:15-17).

## THE COMPLETE PICTURE

One of our favorite family Christmas gifts is a jigsaw puzzle. However many pieces there are, we always follow the same process in assembling them. First, we identify and separate all the outer edge pieces and connect them. Inevitably, in scrutinizing the remaining pieces, we do not think it possible that some of them even belong to the puzzle we are putting together. Could they have been included in error? Placing these difficult pieces to one side, we then begin to assemble the more easily identifiable pieces and compose the picture, the outer edge pieces forming a sure basis from which to work. The more complete the picture becomes, the easier it is to place the pieces we thought were incorrectly included. Large areas of uniformly colored sky, water, or segments devoid of distinguishing features can present a challenge, but over time and after deep contemplation, we complete the picture with satisfaction.

Many similarities exist between assembling a jigsaw puzzle and learning the gospel. The outer edges are comparable to the fundamental doctrines and principles. Once we have these in place, we can build piece by piece, truth by truth, a complete picture of the plan of salvation. The teachings that may initially have seemed more difficult to understand eventually drop easily into place as we compile our own catalog of cherished truths. The final pages will only be written and the missing pieces of the puzzle only provided after the manner described in scripture: "Yea, verily I say unto you, in that day when the Lord shall come, he shall reveal all things—Things which have passed, and hidden things which no man knew, things of the earth, by which it was made, and the purpose and the end thereof—Things most precious, things that are above, and things that are beneath, things that are in the earth, and upon the earth, and in heaven" (D&C 101:32-34). The Lord will unveil the complete picture to our view. I can only imagine the satisfaction that will accompany such understanding—to have the answers to puzzles that currently confound us regarding the physical world as well as the workings of heaven.

## THE LIGHT OF THE WORLD

If we do not draw close to him now, how can we expect to be close to him then? Nativity scenes, Christmas carols, gifts, and colorful lights should draw us closer to our Redeemer and guide us to the greater light.

M. Louise Haskins provided a source of inspiration and an insight into the possibilities that exist when she wrote: "I said to the man who stood at the gate of the year, give me a light that I may tread safely into the unknown, and he replied, go out into the darkness and put your hand in the hand of God. That shall be to you better than a light, and safer than a known way" (in *Masterpieces of Religious Verse*, ed. James Dalton Morrison, 1948, 92).

This next Christmas, may we all put our hand in the hand of God and come to know the source of light and truth, for the lights that illuminate the winter sky are symbolic of a greater light. Then we will know that we are heading in the right direction, for he will make things known unto us.

# PART TWO

*Truths*

*Discerned*

# WE SHALL "COME FORTH AS GOLD"

## THE PAINTING

Some years ago, I had a client who, along with his father, was in the secondhand furniture business. They acquired their inventory by attending auctions and estate sales and by clearing unwanted items from homes.

On one occasion, the son contracted to clear the contents of a home following the death of an elderly occupant. Hanging in one of the rooms was a painting. Pausing to examine it, he considered the possibility that one day he might discover an antique or painting of far greater value than the previous owner had realized. But concluding that this painting was not in that category, he removed it, carried it to his vehicle, and put it among the other items, exercising very little care in doing so.

Later, as he and his father were unloading the vehicle, the father picked up the artwork, examined it carefully, and said, "I wish I knew more about paintings and how to tell if they are valuable." The son responded that he was sure this one would not be classified as such. Nevertheless, the father felt it would be worth having the painting checked by a friend who managed an art gallery.

Several days later, the father's friend informed him that the painting was worth at least £12,000 (almost $29,000 in the early 1970s). Excited by the news, the father and son set out for the art gallery to collect the painting. This time they took a blanket in which they carefully wrapped the work of art. On the return trip to their shop, the son held the painting securely in his arms. Their attitude toward what had now become a valuable item to them had dramatically changed. Before, it had no great significance—it was just another picture among many hundreds they had handled. But with its true worth then established, the painting had become quite a different thing to the men, and they were thrilled when it later sold at auction for £12,500.

In telling this story, my client concluded by saying, "I can't imagine why anyone would pay so much for such an ordinary painting."

Clearly, the value he placed on the painting was a function of its monetary worth and not based on his personal appreciation of its artistic merits. Furthermore, though he was grateful to have discovered the painting's worth, it also caused him some consternation. He wondered, Had they previously allowed something of value to elude their notice?

## THE REAL REASON

Such may be the case in the value we put on Christ. Do we really understand our indebtedness to the Savior and appreciate his divinity and power? Or do we view him as merely a fascinating historical figure? Those persons who encountered him during his earthly sojourn wrestled with the same dilemma. We read in John that following his miraculous feeding of the multitude, Jesus found little respite from those who followed him for the wrong reasons:

"When the people therefore saw that Jesus was not there, neither his disciples, they also took shipping, and came to

Capernaum, seeking for Jesus. And when they had found him on the other side of the sea, they said unto him, Rabbi, when camest thou hither?" (John 6:24-25).

The Joseph Smith Translation of John 6:26 offers this additional insight: "Jesus answered them and said, Verily, verily, I say unto you, Ye seek me, not because ye *desire to keep my sayings*, neither because ye saw the miracles, but because ye did eat of the loaves, and were filled" (emphasis added).

How like the experience of the young man and the painting. Many who witnessed the miracles performed by the Savior during his mortal ministry still had only a superficial understanding of who he was. This is substantiated by an incident described in Matthew:

"And when he was come into his own country, he taught them in their synagogue, insomuch that they were astonished, and said, Whence hath this man this wisdom, and these mighty works? Is not this the carpenter's son? is not his mother called Mary? and his brethren, James, and Joses, and Simon, and Judas? And his sisters, are they not all with us? Whence then hath this man all these things?" (Matthew 13:54-56).

## DOING AND KNOWING

It would appear that many who associated with Jesus saw him as a great miracle worker or teacher but not as the Son of God. How do we progress, then, to real understanding? I believe the answer is revealed in the words of the Savior to the Jews: "If any man will do his will, he shall know of the doctrine" (John 7:17).

I am grateful that I was brought up in a home where Christian values were taught and observed, although without benefit of the knowledge of the restoration of the gospel. Later, as I was invited to explore the message of the Restoration, each new doctrine required deep consideration, often resulting in a change of lifestyle. But those changes did not come about as a result of passive belief or mere intellectual assent. The proof was in the doing, in the exercise of faith. As I learned and then tested gospel principles that were new to me, I invariably found them to be true.

## THE LAW OF THE FAST

One example of this process is my initial encounter with the law of the fast. When I began to investigate the Church, my parents were very supportive as I shared with them the details of my newly developing faith. My mother, however, became concerned when I discussed with her my desire to fast for twenty-four hours. She wondered if going without food and drink for that amount of time was wise. Fearing the practice would be detrimental to my health, she was adamant, saying she would not agree to letting me fast while in her home.

I suppose I was less than enthused about not having anything to eat or drink for a full day, and so it was with a feeling of some relief that I reported my mother's objections to my member-missionary, Pamela, informing her that, unfortunately, I would not be able to participate in the fast. Without hesitation, Pamela responded, "We can easily take care of that. I'll arrange with my parents for you to stay at our home for the weekend so that you can fast with us." This was my introduction to the law of the fast. As I continued to observe this law each fast day, I gradually gained a testimony of the benefits and underlying principles of fasting.

The Savior taught, "If any man will do his will, he shall know of the doctrine, whether it be of God, or whether I speak of myself" (John 7:17). It is true. When we implement a principle of truth in our lives, we gain a testimony of the divine source of that truth. President Brigham Young expressed his belief that "every principle God has revealed carries its own convictions of its truth to the human mind" (*Journal of Discourses*, 9:149). Moreover, a practice often becomes easier as we follow it. In this regard, President Heber J. Grant often quoted Emerson, who said, "That which we persist in doing becomes easier to do; not that the nature of the thing is changed, but our power to do is increased." In my introduction to the gospel, I found it to be true that there is a direct relationship between obedience and testimony, between doing and knowing.

## TITHING, A DIVINE LAW

I can vividly recall a sunny Sunday afternoon in July 1959 when Pamela and I were walking and talking together. I was contemplating becoming a member of the Church, and Pamela said to me, "I can't remember the missionaries teaching you about tithing."

"What is tithing?" I asked.

Pamela responded by explaining that in obedience to God's law and as an expression of their gratitude for all that our Heavenly Father has given them, members give 10 percent of their income to the Church.

There have been only a few moments in my life when I have felt faint as a result of shock, and this was one of them.

"Ten percent!" I echoed. "That's impossible. There's no way I could afford to pay tithing."

Pamela calmly replied, "My father does. He has a wife and four children, and his income is less than yours." She also mentioned another family I had come to know in the branch, informing me that they had six children and were living on less money than I. This proved to be a useful challenge to me. If they could manage, I thought, then so could I.

Eleven years later, faced with a real test of my commitment to that law, I realized that I had developed great faith through the payment of tithing. It was no longer simply a matter of money to me. In response to that test, I exercised my faith and was blessed for it (see Malachi 3:10).

## THE SABBATH DAY

Prior to my introduction to the restored gospel, I spent much of my time playing soccer, including games on Sundays. I had been brought up to have respect for the Lord's day, but I saw nothing wrong with playing soccer on the Sabbath. It wasn't until I came in contact with the Church that Sunday soccer became an issue. Withdrawing from the Sunday league team was a significant sacrifice, but by doing so I exercised my faith and was rewarded with a testimony of the principle, not to mention associated blessings. Observing the Sabbath contributed substantially to my conversion.

Three years later, when work commenced on building a chapel in Norwich, I also withdrew from the Saturday league team so I could work on the new chapel. The mist of self-interest that had previously restricted my vision was beginning to disperse, and a new panoramic view was emerging, bringing with it a deeper appreciation for, and an increasing love of, life.

## DISCIPLESHIP

By surrendering to the doctrines and practices of the Church, we become disciples of Christ. He said, "If ye continue in my word, then are ye my disciples indeed; And ye shall know the truth, and the truth shall make you free" (John 8:31-32). One could interpret the first part of this verse to mean, "If ye continue to live in harmony with my doctrine." This reinforces the relationship between doing and knowing. I remember hearing Elder Dallin H. Oaks once define this process by saying that "testimony is to know and to feel, conversion is to do and to become."

*Knowing* and *feeling* are essential elements of conversion, but our progress will be flawed without our *doing* and *becoming.* Ascending to our greatest potential and achieving the full measure of our creation is not made possible simply by the things we have done. The ultimate test is what we become.

A checklist of achievements will not qualify us for the greatest gift of God. Participation in ordinances and a perfunctory approach toward making and keeping covenants will not suffice, unless we ascend above temporal temptations and become also "partakers of the divine nature" (2 Peter 1:4). We ought to "pray unto the Father with all the energy of heart, that ye may be filled with this love, which he hath bestowed upon all who are true followers of his Son, Jesus Christ; that ye may become the sons [and daughters] of God; that when he shall appear we shall be like him" (Moroni 7:48).

Yes, testimony is to know and to feel, conversion is to do and to ultimately become like the Son.

## PHYSICAL AND SPIRITUAL WELL-BEING

An analogy exists between engaging in a physical fitness program and working to apply gospel principles in our lives. When we regularly engage in physical activities, the benefits may not be dramatically apparent. However, when illness, injury, or lack of desire interrupt our fitness programs for a prolonged period, we experience great difficulty in regaining the level of fitness we previously enjoyed. Some become so discouraged by the required struggle that they settle for a lesser level of fitness.

This can be true also of maintaining spiritual fitness; the benefits may not always be noticeable. This may cause some to question the reality of the doctrine, and thus lose their faith and discontinue their Church activity. Those who work their way back to spiritual fitness usually discover a greater appreciation for the gospel. Others slip away and walk no more with the Lord.

## "WILL YE ALSO GO AWAY?"

The book of John in the New Testament contains an interesting account of an exchange between Jesus and his disciples. Following a dissertation in which Jesus expounded doctrine that was difficult to accept, "Many therefore of His disciples, when they had heard this, said, This is an hard saying; who can hear it? When Jesus knew in himself that his disciples murmured at it, he said unto them, Doth this offend you?" Apparently it did, for "from that time many of his disciples went back, and walked no more with him." Challenging the twelve to remain faithful, Jesus asked them pointedly, "Will ye also go away?" Affirming his faith and determination to remain true, Peter answered for himself and the others: "Lord, to whom shall we go? thou hast the words of eternal life. And we believe and are sure that thou art that Christ, the Son of the living God" (John 6:60-61, 66-69). Peter had received a witness of the truthfulness of the Savior's words, which had been "written not with ink, but with the Spirit of the living God; not in tables of stone, but in fleshy tables of the heart" (2 Corinthians 3:3).

## TREASURES OF KNOWLEDGE

The promise to those who live in harmony with the Word of Wisdom and who walk "in obedience to the commandments" is that they "shall receive health in their navel and marrow to their bones" (D&C 89:18). The admonition to "keep and do these sayings, walking in obedience to the commandments," is significant. Verse 19 adds another dimension that to some may seem almost unrelated to what is often seen exclusively as a health code. But the verse contains the great key and link between doing and knowing: "And shall find wisdom and great treasures of knowledge, even hidden treasures."

Some doctrines may not be easily proven in practical

terms. Nevertheless, I believe the key that opens the way to our understanding of the plan of salvation and to our testimony of the efficacy of the Savior's atonement in our own lives is found by faithful adherence to gospel principles.

## WE WILL PROVE THEM

In the premortal world we learned that the earth on which we live was provided as a dwelling place to "prove [us] herewith to see if [we] will do all things whatsoever the Lord [our] God shall command [us]" (Abraham 3:25). This is the process by which the Lord tests our faithfulness. After revealing to us gospel truths, the Lord tests our hearts and minds relative to our new knowledge. As we overcome a trial, the principle we have thus tested is indelibly stamped upon our souls. Our understandings and our hearts are purified in the process, almost as gold. But we are required to walk much of the way by faith. Mormon explained that he did not include in his records all that Jesus had taught in order "to try [our] faith, and if it shall so be that they shall believe these things then shall the greater things be made manifest unto them" (3 Nephi 26:9).

The story of Job illustrates how this works. Job was stripped of all that would seem to be precious. But by continuing to live righteously during his period of testing, he discovered something even more precious. This beleaguered man declared his faith that God "knoweth the way that I take: when he hath tried me, I shall come forth as gold" (Job 23:10).

A testimony of the restored gospel is like a fabric, with divine doctrine and eternal principles woven together to create a pattern of exquisite beauty. But only those who follow the prescribed way of weaving the fabric—living the gospel—may perceive its beauty. By no other means can we fully develop the potential of the human soul. As we do the Lord's will, we really can know of the truth of the doctrine, and after our faith and trust have been tried, we too will "come forth as gold."

# THEY SHALL LEARN
# WISDOM

## PATTERNS OF LEARNING

I commenced my printing apprenticeship when I was sixteen years old. This involved gaining practical experience by working in the printing department of a food-packaging and distribution company and attending college classes. The apprenticeship was to last five years.

On my first day at the printing facility, the supervisor gave me a tour, introducing me to the personnel, the printing presses, and the products.

After the tour, he led me to a large press and announced that this was where I would be working. I naively concluded that I would be given charge of this machine. My illusion was quickly shattered when I was introduced to Stanley, a mature, highly qualified machine minder. Stanley explained to me how the printing press operated and warned me of the hazards involved in working with moving machinery. Then he entrusted me to the care of Ted, his assistant, who was responsible for the manual work associated with operating the press. This included stacking paper into the machine's feed mechanism. Ted showed me how to fan air between the sheets of paper so they would not cling together and impede their progress through the printing cycle.

Having the benefit of many years experience, my trainer tackled the task with ease. When given the opportunity to follow his example, I could not understand why the glossy sheets of paper had not slipped from his fingers as they did from mine. Ted had to reshuffle the paper before it was suitable for use.

Eventually, I mastered the techniques he taught me, spending most of my time over a six-month period handling plain paper at one end of the press or the finished product at the other end.

Meanwhile, at college, I was learning the more technical aspects of printing. The contrast between these two activities led me to conclude that those responsible for my practical training were not allowing me to progress in a manner commensurate with my newly gained knowledge. It seemed to me as though the prolonged period of handling paper was simply an attempt to occupy my time. Looking back, I realize that I needed to master the fundamental skills if I was to ever become a proficient printer.

This principle applies not just to learning a trade or developing a talent. It is the pattern by which we acquire all knowledge. The scriptures describe this process in these words: "For behold, thus saith the Lord God: I will give unto the children of men line upon line, precept upon precept, here a little and there a little; and blessed are those who hearken unto my precepts, and lend an ear unto my counsel, for they shall learn wisdom; for unto him that receiveth I will give more; and from them that shall say, We have enough, from them shall be taken away even that which they have" (2 Nephi 28:30).

I am convinced that when we say, "We have enough," we

lose not only the truths we reject but also the truths to which our souls once resonated.

Just as a great musician begins with scales and a champion athlete with basic physical skills, so must we start on the lower rungs in our quest for spiritual ascendancy. Regarding this principle, the Prophet Joseph Smith taught: "When you climb up a ladder, you must begin at the bottom, and ascend step by step, until you arrive at the top; and so it is with the principles of the gospel—you must begin with the first, and go on until you learn all the principles of exaltation. But it will be a great while after you have passed through the veil before you will have learned them. It is not all to be comprehended in this world; it will be a great work to learn our salvation and exaltation even beyond the grave" (*History of the Church*, 6:306-07).

## THE VALUE OF EXPERIENCE

Members of each generation must discover truth for themselves. When we are young, our parents and others of previous generations often appear to be outdated in their thinking and behind the times. We assume the things we discover when we are young are new and previously unknown. I vividly recall having such an attitude as a teenager.

As previously mentioned, when I was seventeen, I was a member of a musical band called a "skiffle" group, which were all the rage during my teenage years.

Ever interested in my activities, my father asked if he could attend one of our group's practice sessions. I happily agreed, and my colleagues did not object. The evening Dad attended the band practice, we performed three numbers and then invited his observations. He offered some helpful insights that we were pleased to receive, but he then made a suggestion that we rejected.

Vocally impersonating the sound of a bass, he demonstrated

how the rhythm might give shape and definition to the music. We thanked him but dismissed his advice as irrelevant to the style of music we were playing. Only later, as I progressed to playing dance music, did I realize and acknowledge to my father that his counsel relating to the fundamental rhythm of our music had been correct. He had not previously pressed the matter, realizing that I would eventually discover this for myself.

So often, in our teenage years particularly, we reject wise counsel and sound instruction, assuming we know better than those who are trying to help us. This occurs not only in temporal but in spiritual matters. As we humble ourselves and receive the word with all readiness of heart, our capacity to understand is enlarged, and we qualify to be taught by the voice of the Spirit. For thus do the doctrines of the priesthood distill upon our souls as the dews from heaven (see D&C 121:45).

Wise parents and leaders will exercise patience when working with youth. Young people need to be nourished with milk before meat, and they should not be expected to achieve levels of performance beyond that which they are capable.

It is wonderful to observe a young man or a young woman catch the vision of their potential as a child of God. It is particularly refreshing to see a young man begin to recognize the significance of the Aaronic Priesthood duties he is privileged to perform and to witness the remarkable transformation that takes place in his life when he displaces disinterest with diligence and replaces reticence with reverence.

## A FAMILY OUTING TO THE BEACH

When our son, Kevin, was old enough to walk with support, Pamela and I decided it would be a wonderful experience to introduce him to the North Sea. (Our home was located only twenty miles from the east coast of England.) The motivation to do so was generated by fond recollections and unforgettable memories of our own childhood experiences at the beach.

We were excited to embark on what we anticipated would be a great adventure for our son. Our destination was the coastal town of Hemsby, where a large stretch of golden sand stretched from grass-covered sand dunes down to the seashore. I carried Kevin in my arms over the sand until we located a suitable place to settle and where Pamela spread a large bath towel on the sand.

Kevin was content to sit on the towel, and all my attempts to encourage him to walk on the sand were unsuccessful. He was happy to allow grains of sand to run between his fingers but only from the security of the area covered by the towel. Each time I took hold of his hands and tried to entice him to walk on the sand, he found the instability beneath his feet disconcerting and quickly returned to what he considered a secure area.

We had anticipated that one of the highlights of the day would be Kevin's introduction to the sea, but as I picked him up and walked toward the water, he became fearful and began to wriggle in my arms. The closer we got to the water, the more distraught he became. He recoiled from the waves and began to cry. At first I didn't understand what was the matter, but then it dawned on me. He was frightened. The majesty of the sea, which I found so stimulating, was overwhelming to him.

Recognizing the reason for his distress, I sat with him on the sand with the shoreline behind us. Kevin quickly regained his composure and was content to play with what had now become his familiar friend, the sand. Still wanting to introduce him to the water, I stood up after a time and took him by his hands, holding him so his toes just reached the sand made firm by the outgoing tide. Then I walked slowly backward, toward the water, stopping at a point where the spent waves lapped gently around our feet. Kevin enjoyed this sensation and kicked at the water with his feet. As he continued to play, I gradually turned him seaward until he realized he was playing in the great mass of water that had initially caused him so much fear. Although he was not yet mature enough to comprehend the magnitude of the sea, this introduction was comfortable enough to invite further exploration.

In similar manner, children need exposure to things of a spiritual nature. Unfortunately, the faith of parents does not automatically transfer to their children. If our little ones are to acquire testimonies, we must instill gospel ideals and principles in their hearts in their formative years. For the years of childhood and youth are times of preparation and discovery in which character is molded and seeds of faith are sown. If nourished, these seeds will bring forth fruit throughout our lives.

## A PARABLE FOR MOTHERS

A parable for mothers, first published in *Stepping Stones* magazine in 1946, beautifully describes the influence and objectives of parenthood:

> A young mother set her foot on the path of life. "Is the way long?" she asked. And the guide said, "Yes, and the way is hard. And you will be old before you reach the end of it. But the end will be better than the beginning."
>
> But the young mother was happy, and she would not believe that anything could be better than these years. So she played with her children and gathered flowers for them along the way. And the sun shone on them, and life was good, and the young mother cried, "Nothing will ever be lovelier than this!"
>
> Then came night and storm, and the path was dark, and the children shook with fear and cold. But the mother drew close to them and covered them with her

mantle, and the children said, "We are not afraid, Mother, for you are near; and no harm can come to us."

And the mother said, "This is better than the brightness of day, for I have taught my children courage."

And the morning came, and there was a hill ahead, and the children climbed and grew weary, and the mother was weary.

But at last she said to the children, "A little patience, and we are there."

So the children climbed, and when they reached the top, they said, "We could not have done this without you, Mother."

And that night the mother looked up at the stars, and said, "This is a better day than the last, for my children have learned fortitude in the face of hardship. Yesterday I gave them courage, today I gave them strength."

And the next day came strange clouds which darkened the earth—clouds of war and hate and evil, and the children groped and stumbled. The mother said, "Look up; lift your eyes to the light."

And the children looked, and saw above the clouds an everlasting light, and it guided them and brought them beyond the darkness.

And that night the mother said, "This is the best day of all, for I have shown my children God."

And the days went on and the weeks and the months and the years, and the mother grew aged, and she was little and bent.

But the children were tall and strong and walked with courage. And when the way was hard, they lifted her over the rough places.

At last they came to a hill, and beyond the hill they could see a shining road and golden gates, and they flung wide.

And the mother said, "I have reached the end of my

journey. And now I know that the end is better than the beginning, for my children can walk alone and their children after them."

And the children said, "You will always walk with us, Mother!"

And they stood and watched her walk through the golden gates, and the gates closed after her. And they said, "We cannot now see our mother, but she is with us still—she is a living presence."

For those who follow the everlasting light, the end will truly be better than the beginning. I find it reassuring that after Job had endured his tribulations, "the Lord blessed the latter end of Job more than his beginning" (Job 42:12).

Some find it difficult to appreciate things that are eternal when they are surrounded by that which is temporal. However, the soul that is spiritually attuned reaches naturally out beyond the restrictions of mortality to the promises of eternity. Through the agency of the Holy Ghost we are able to look beyond this worldly sphere, using our mortal experiences to find types and shadows of spiritual realities—to visualize the invisible and discover things hidden from the natural eye. The Book of Mormon teaches us that gaining spiritual awareness is a gradual process: "And when they shall have received this, which is expedient that they should have first, to try their faith, and if it shall so be that they shall believe these things then shall the greater things be made manifest unto them" (3 Nephi 26:9).

The Apostle Paul described this spiritual awareness when he wrote: "The things of God knoweth no man, but the Spirit of the God. Now we have received, not the spirit of the world, but the spirit which is of God; that we might know the things that are freely given to us of God. Which things also we speak, not in the words which man's wisdom teacheth, but which the

Holy Ghost teacheth; comparing spiritual things with spiritual. But the natural man receiveth not the things of the Spirit of God: for they are foolishness unto him: neither can he know them, because they are spiritually discerned" (1 Corinthians 2:11-14).

## BECOMING SERVANTS OF THE LORD

One of the most significant lessons I have learned is how, under the influence of the Holy Spirit, individuals from diverse backgrounds and holding different perspectives can achieve complete unity in even the most complex situations—in Church council meetings. This demonstrates the potential that exists to gain understanding from the true source of wisdom as described in Job 32:8, "But there is a spirit in man: and the inspiration of the Almighty giveth them understanding." It has been encouraging to me to know that the Lord is mindful of his servants. He addressed priesthood holders in the early Church by saying, "Hearken, O ye elders of my church whom I have called" (D&C 41:3). All who serve in his Church are called of God through what the Prophet Joseph Smith called "prophecy" (Articles of Faith 1:5)—that is to say by inspiration directed by the Holy Spirit. Church work is not easy. It is, in fact, very demanding, and unless we know that the source of our calling is divine, we are susceptible to discouragement. However, when we know that we have been called of God, we can say as did Nephi, "I will go and do the things which the Lord hath commanded, for I know that the Lord giveth no commandments unto the children of men, save he shall prepare a way for them that they may accomplish the thing which he commandeth them" (1 Nephi 3:7).

In the introduction of his letters to the Romans, Corinthians, Galatians, Ephesians, Philippians, Colossians, and to Timothy and Titus, the Apostle Paul affirmed that he knew from whence his call came by declaring himself "Paul, a servant of Jesus Christ, *called* to be an apostle." That certainty enabled him to boldly affirm, "We are troubled on every side, yet not distressed; we are perplexed, but not in despair. Persecuted, but not forsaken; cast down, but not destroyed" (2 Corinthians 4:8-9). Having a confirmation of the source of our call, we are able to be buoyant through buffeting and valiant through adversity.

That men and women are called to positions of responsibility by divine inspiration is one of the distinctive characteristics of the true and living Church. The Lord's Church is governed by other unique principles. The Doctrine and Covenants mentions several of these principles: "Behold I give unto you a *commandment* that ye shall assemble yourselves together" (D&C 41:2; emphasis added). This might apply to a bishopric or presidency and to meetings in every sphere of priesthood and auxiliary leadership, including stake, ward, and family councils. The purpose of such gatherings is to "agree upon my word," or "my will." As each participant in the presidency or council shares insights and makes suggestions, acting out of a desire to discover the will of the Lord, unity is achieved and difficult decisions are made. We set aside personal preferences as we seek to act according to the Lord's will. D&C 41:3 emphasizes the importance of prayer in this process: "And by the prayer of your faith ye shall receive my law, that ye may know how to govern my church and have all things right before me." This process is not restrictive or inhibiting. Decisions made in such an environment are not based on the wisdom of man but are inspired and approved of God.

Jacob taught this principle in the following manner: "Wherefore, brethren, seek not to counsel the Lord, but to take counsel from his hand. For behold, ye yourselves know that he counseleth in wisdom, and in justice, and in great mercy, over all his works" (Jacob 4:10). In business meetings and in secular committees or organizations, we have a tendency to selfishly promote our own point of view or preference and to defend positions appeal to us. But in Church government and leadership responsibilities, we need to be motivated by a desire to be the Lord's servants and to do his will. One of the benefits of such service is the friendship that develops between those who labor together in his service. I have a deep appreciation for all those with whom I have served. Acting in the Lord's name under the direction of the Holy Spirit has created an everlasting bond among us.

Whether we are fulfilling parental responsibilities or serving in a Church assignment, we have access to the greatest source of learning and the highest form of instruction—God, who is omniscient. Awakened to these possibilities, we can, like Jesus, increase "in wisdom and stature, and in favour with God and man" (Luke 2:52).

# A MIGHTY CHANGE

# OF HEART

## MY INTRODUCTION TO THE RESTORED GOSPEL

A scriptural passage that evokes tender feelings within me is recorded in the book of Alma, wherein Alma expresses his feelings in these words: "And behold, when I see many of my brethren truly penitent, and coming to the Lord their God, then is my soul filled with joy; then do I remember what the Lord has done for me, yea, even that he hath heard my prayer; yea, then do I remember his merciful arm which he extended towards me" (Alma 29:10).

Looking back on my life, I can see how the Lord's influence prepared and positioned me so that I would be reawakened to the purposes of our existence and gain an insight into our true potential.

The year 1959 was significant for me. At a time when I should have been giving priority to my studies, I was distracted by my interest in playing soccer and my involvement as a guitarist and vocalist with a band. Taking note of my lack of commitment and resulting mediocre grades, one of my college instructors tried to capture my attention and stimulate my interest by telling me, "You are wasting my time and yours." At that time in my life, I found sports and entertainment to be more stimulating than my studies.

During this time, one of my friends suggested that dancing lessons might provide us an interesting diversion. His suggestion received unanimous acceptance, and shortly thereafter, seventeen young men presented themselves at the Norman School of Dancing located at All Saints Green, Norwich. A young female dance instructor, at first somewhat overwhelmed by the number and makeup of our group, greeted us. She proceeded to apprise us of the rules and regulations we would be expected to observe, mentioning particularly the formal dances, which the school sponsored on Friday and Saturday nights, and which we would be allowed to attend only when she felt we were qualified.

Several weeks passed before our instructor granted us permission to attend one of the formal dances, which were held in a popular, pleasant venue. Mr. Norman, the school's proprietor, provided the music and acted as master of ceremonies and disc jockey.

## FIRST ENCOUNTER

One evening, as I was standing at the side of the dance floor, a friend pointed to a young lady dancing across the hall from where we were and said, "If there's one girl I would like to dance with, it is that girl over there." Observing the young lady, I thought, *If he would, I will.* As the music for the next dance began, I walked over to where the young lady was sitting and asked if she would dance with me. She accepted my invitation, and we danced to the rhythm of a slow fox-trot.

The young lady was an accomplished ballroom dancer and must have found my newly developing skills distinctly awkward. In the course of our conversation, she informed me that she was a Mormon. I was not familiar with the word and wondered if it might be a contagious condition. (I am pleased to report that it is.)

The dance ended, and I escorted the young lady to her seat and then returned to where my friends were assembled. I was intrigued by what she had told me and said to my friends, "That girl I just danced with is a Mormon. What do you suppose that means?"

They responded almost in unison, saying, "That's great! You can have as many wives as you like."

I was the only one in our group who had never heard of Mormons, and I was puzzled by their response. I didn't know what they meant by having more than one wife, and such an idea wasn't consistent with the favorable impression the young lady had made on me.

Just then, Mr. Norman announced the next dance, and music once again filled the air. I walked over and asked the same young woman for another dance, but she refused my invitation. She was obviously unimpressed by our previous encounter, which on reflection was understandable, since I had tried to steal a kiss during our dance. My behavior was inappropriate, and even though my sensitivity to sacred things had not yet been fully awakened, I felt embarrassed. I rejoined my friends without divulging what had taken place.

Over the next few weeks, I attended several dances at the Norman School of Dancing. One night while conversing with a friend, the young lady who had declined my invitation approached me and said, "I apologize for refusing to dance with you. If on a future occasion you wish to dance with me again, I would be happy to do so."

I arrogantly concluded that this change of attitude had something to do with me. But, as I learned later, her apology was prompted by a lesson given in her branch "Mutual Improvement Association" organization. Her teacher had described to the class how difficult it is for a young man to find the courage to invite a young lady to dance. The young woman's apology was motivated by obedience to the teacher.

Without hesitation, I took advantage of this opportunity and requested the pleasure of her company in a dance. Throughout the evening I repeated the invitation, learning more about her each time we danced and becoming increasingly fascinated by her.

## THE SACRAMENT MEETING

I inquired if there might be some other opportunity to see her. She responded that Monday was family home evening, Tuesday she attended MIA, Wednesday was Relief Society, Thursday she taught in Primary, and Friday she had a church leadership meeting. She had another meeting on Saturday, and on Sunday she attended church worship meetings.

I interrupted her to ask if she had time between any of these activities that I could spend with her. After pondering this question, she responded by saying, "Well, there is some time on Sunday afternoon between meetings when I could meet you if you wish." I acknowledged that this would be suitable, and we agreed to meet on Earlham Road, Norwich. After our parting, I looked forward excitedly to our rendezvous.

It was a sunny Sunday afternoon. I boarded the number 79 bus and alighted at the location we had agreed to meet. She was there, and we walked and talked together until the young lady posed a question, "Would you like to meet my parents?" I wondered why. What was the significance of this question?

I asked a question in response, "Where are they?"

"They are in that building," she replied, pointing to a nearby small chapel.

I replied by saying, "You need to know that I have no interest in religion."

She responded, "I did not ask you about religion. I asked if you would like to meet my parents."

Not wishing to be misunderstood, I reiterated my position: "I have no intention of attending any church meetings."

"I never mentioned church meetings," she replied. "I asked if you would like to meet my parents."

"I have no desire to get involved with a church. It holds no appeal for me," I said.

"Do you want to meet my parents or not?"

"As long as you understand!"

Satisfied that I had communicated my feelings, I accompanied her into the building through a side door that led into a hall at the rear of the chapel. There I was introduced to her father, mother, brother, and sisters. Approximately twenty other people were in the hall.

We spent the afternoon conversing, then at five minutes to six in the evening the sound of organ music drifted into the hall from the chapel. The young lady said good-bye to me and walked with her family and the others into the chapel. I was alone and pondered what I should do. Concluding that I could probably tolerate one meeting, I joined the congregation in the chapel. Sitting beside my friend on a hard wood bench, I whispered to her, "How long will this last?"

Her response stunned me. "Ninety minutes," she said.

*Ninety minutes!* I thought. *This is probably going to be the most boring ninety minutes of my life.* But I was scarcely conscious of the passage of time. I cannot remember who spoke, and I do not recall the specific words spoken, but what I heard I had heard before, and it was not in mortality. It was strange to listen, for the first time, to principles that I recognized and already believed. Looking back with the knowledge I now have, I feel as if the veil parted momentarily and I was remembering what I had been taught in the premortal existence.

Much later, I discovered this scriptural insight: "Even before they were born, they, with many others, received their first lessons in the world of spirits and were prepared to come forth in the due time of the Lord to labor in his vineyard for the salvation of the souls of men" (D&C 138:56).

## MEETING THE MISSIONARIES

As I have since pondered what happened and reflected on what I felt during those moments, I have come to recognize the significance of that first encounter with the Latter-day Saints. But as remarkable as that experience was, it did not bring an immediate conversion or create within me a desire to change my lifestyle. But my interest in the young lady was growing, prompting me to seek more opportunities to be in her company.

During a subsequent discussion in which I was trying to determine what opportunities might be available for me to see her, she suggested the possibility of my escorting her to a meeting held Sunday evenings following the sacrament service. She and other district missionaries met then with the full-time missionaries in a family home to receive training relevant to their responsibilities. She suggested that I could walk her home afterward. Motivated by a desire to be with her, I was susceptible to almost any reasonable proposal, and agreed.

Initially, I merely sat in the corner of the room and observed as the training exercises were conducted. During the third or fourth meeting that I attended, Elder Baker asked if I could assist the instructors. I asked him what he had in mind. He replied that it was difficult to conduct effective training for some elements necessary to become a successful missionary without demonstrating how this should be accomplished. He asked if I would be willing to take the part of the investigator. I agreed and was exposed to the missionary discussions in the process.

During one of the discussions, while Elder Baker was examining the principle of prayer, he asked me if I would offer a prayer. When I said I didn't know what was required, Elder Baker explained the four components of prayer:

1. Address Heavenly Father
2. Express gratitude for blessings received
3. Ask for guidance, and articulate needs
4. Close in the name of Jesus Christ

At this point Elder Baker placed his hand on my arm while moving from a seated position on a chair to his knees. His momentum brought me to a kneeling position at his side, and I found myself for the first time in my life offering a personal prayer. This experience drew me closer to spiritual realities, but two other memorable moments helped me make a significant transition in my life.

## MEMORABLE MOMENTS

I had walked the young lady home one evening, and we were engaged in conversation when she surprised me by saying, "You do realize I would never consider marrying you!" She had obviously sensed that my intentions were becoming increasingly more serious, and the statement startled me. She continued, "Unless, of course, you could take me to the temple." I did not immediately understand the significance of these words, but I sensed how important it was to this young woman.

The second memorable moment occurred a few nights later. As we were parting she said, "You do understand that I love the gospel more than I love you, for without the gospel our love would be nothing." It was as if a light had been switched on. It occurred to me that I had been trying to entice her away from the very thing that had made her what she was— the gospel. How could I love her and reject the lifestyle and beliefs that had made her so special?

Over the following weeks I attended church regularly, associated with her family, enjoyed the spirit that permeated their
home, and was taught the basic principles of the gospel.
During this period, I learned the law of the fast and came to
discover the blessings that result from complying with the
principle of tithing.

This intriguing young woman was named Pamela Wilson.
We first met on April 11, 1959, and I was baptized just over
four months later, on August 16, 1959. We were married on
March 24, 1962.

Once my life was illuminated by the light of the everlasting
gospel and I had learned that I was a child of God, my perception of myself and my potential changed. What happened was
profound. I began to achieve distinction in the courses of study
I had once been failing. My instructor asked many times what
had happened to me, but he was never able to understand my
explanation. The principal of the college invited me to be an
evening instructor, and my life was elevated to a higher level of
expectation and achievement. I shall ever be grateful to Pamela
for introducing me to the principles of the restored gospel and
helping to make possible the mighty change of heart that I
experienced.

One of the things that sustained me while I was learning
the gospel was the admirable lives of those who had already
accepted the message of the restoration. Pamela, her parents,
and the members of her family were living examples of the
gospel in action. The power of their example provided the life-
line to which I clung while discovering and exploring the
doctrine for myself.

Even the Book of Mormon, which has become a cherished
companion and a fundamental source of my faith, did not
immediately capture my interest. I was initially attracted to and

sustained by friendship and feelings before I developed sufficient comprehension to grasp the truth of the book's message.

I had originally been skeptical of what I perceived as
extremes of religious expression. At first hearing, the account
of Joseph's encounter with the Father and the Son in the
Sacred Grove certainly fell into this category for me. But logic
helped. The accounts in the Holy Bible clearly showed that
God reveals himself through heavenly manifestations. *Why not
today as in times past?* I asked myself.

Weighing possibilities and considering the options
enabled me to explore as never before the realities of true religion. Gradually, I came to accept Joseph Smith's visions as
plausible. The Holy Spirit then bore witness of their verity. In
time, I came to know in the depths of my soul things that I was
otherwise unable to explain or incapable of expressing. Such
things are not learned by logic or perceived through human
intellect. They may be known only through the ministration of
the Holy Spirit and divine inspiration. My introduction to the
message of the restoration and my initial search were prompted
by feelings; now, forty years later, my faith is sustained by the
feelings I have about the things that I know.

In the depth of our souls, we know things that we are
unable to explain or express. We know these spiritual truths
only through the promptings of the Holy Spirit. Enjoying the
companionship of the Spirit, having caring friends, taking
advantage of opportunities to serve, and being "nourished by
the good word of God" (Jacob 6:7; see also Moroni 6:4) have
strengthened my faith and established my testimony.

I acknowledge the hand of the Lord and his influence in
my life. My heart is filled with joy when I see others uniting
themselves with the Church and the Lord through baptism.
"Then do I remember what the Lord has done for me."

# CLEAVE UNTO
# THE COVENANTS

## COVENANTS AND CALLINGS

One of the many lessons I learned at the feet of my parents was the importance of making and keeping promises. I have benefited from this aspect of their teaching in every facet of my life. It provoked within me an irrepressible desire to fulfill obligations and meet commitments. Another dimension of commitment was added when I was baptized, as the most important promises in my life were converted into covenants.

## PRECIOUS PROMISES

The words of this poem portray a poignant message:

*The world is rife with promises*
*that are fast and falsely spoken.*
*For man in his deceptive way*
*knows his promise can be broken.*
*But when God makes a promise,*
*it remains forever true.*
*For everything God promises*
*he unalterably will do.*
*So when you're disillusioned,*

*and every hope is blighted,*
*Recall the promises of God,*
*and your faith will be relighted.*
Helen Steiner Rice

We can trust in the Lord. The scriptures declare his promises, and his works testify of their truth. I take particular assurance from these words: "For the eternal purposes of the Lord shall roll on, until all his promises shall be fulfilled" (Mormon 8:22).

Within twenty-four months of my baptism, I was called to serve as the age-group counselor in the district Young Men presidency with Brother Wheeler as president. When the call was extended, the district president, Jeffrey F. Packe, advised me that I would be required to attend branch conference meetings. He indicated that my first opportunity would be to attend the Gorleston Branch conference two weeks later.

On the morning of the conference, I traveled to my home unit and attended priesthood and Sunday School meetings. Following the meetings, I walked to a nearby telephone kiosk and placed a call to the information number for local rail services. I asked when the next train would depart for Great Yarmouth, which was the railway station nearest to my desired destination. Following a pause, the rail clerk informed me that the next train for Great Yarmouth would not leave until 7:00 the following morning. In a shocked state, I said, "But I need to travel to Great Yarmouth today."

In a calm tone of voice, he replied, "I am sorry, sir."

Replacing the telephone handset, I hurried to the bus stop and boarded a bus for home. Arriving home, I wheeled my bicycle from the garden shed and set off for Gorleston, which was twenty-five miles away. Although I had cycled this route before as a teenager, on those occasions I had had the benefit of a racing cycle and was clad in appropriate clothing. Wearing a suit and riding a basic bicycle was a vastly different experience.

I eventually arrived at the meeting house and walked into the chapel. President Packe was standing at the pulpit. He observed what a wonderful conference it had been and then announced the closing hymn and that Brother Kenneth Johnson would pronounce the benediction. Following the hymn, I walked to the pulpit and offered the benediction, then greeted those on the stand and members in the congregation without mentioning that I had arrived at the close of the meeting—or my mode of transportation. Returning to my bicycle, I mounted and pedaled the twenty-five-mile return journey home. The following days brought painful reminders of my expedition, and I was grateful that my daily occupation did not require me to be seated.

Reflecting upon those events has helped me to identify the driving force behind my actions. The covenants I made at baptism and the sacred promises I made when receiving the Melchizedek Priesthood compel me to do all in my power to diligently honor every assignment and obligation, and to accept every opportunity presented to me. The words of the baptismal covenant as explained by Alma are of great import to me. After explaining the responsibility the people would take upon themselves as members of Christ's Church, Alma said: "Now I say unto you, if this be the desire of your hearts, what have you against being baptized in the name of the Lord, as a witness before him that ye have entered into a covenant with him, *that ye will serve him and keep his commandments, that he may pour out his Spirit more abundantly upon you?*" (Mosiah 18:10; emphasis added).

## SERVING WITH FULL PURPOSE OF HEART

My next assignment was to attend the Colchester Branch conference, which involved traveling sixty-two miles. I shall

ever be grateful for the sequence in which these two assignments came because I would have suffered even more severe
consequences had I found it necessary to cycle that even longer
distance.

After carefully checking the train schedule, I arrived at the
railway station in good time and enjoyed a pleasant journey
through the beautiful green countryside and farmlands of East
Anglia. This was my first visit to Colchester, and I had not
thought to inquire about the location of the meeting place.
This was particularly critical because meetings were held in
rented accommodations, as there were no LDS chapels in the
area.

Leaving the station, I walked in the direction of town centre, which was indicated on a street sign. After walking a short
distance, I came to a major road that bypassed the town to
keep traffic out of the residential and shopping center of the
community. There, a police officer was standing on a raised
wooden platform in the middle of a busy intersection directing
traffic. It was difficult to maneuver through the traffic, but after
some effort I reached the platform on which the officer was
standing. I managed to attract his attention without being able
to have eye contact, since his concentration had to remain
focused on the traffic that continued to converge at the
intersection.

When I asked him if he knew where the meeting place of
The Church of Jesus Christ of Latter-day Saints was located, he
appeared to be annoyed. While still using hand signals to
direct the steady stream of traffic, he nodded somewhat irrita-
bly toward a nearby church building. In an impatient tone of
voice, he said, "Why don't you ask there?" I negotiated my way
back through the traffic to the safety of the foot path and
headed for the church building.

As I entered the grounds, I observed a man using a broom

to sweep up confetti from the driveway. Whether it was that task that had angered him or my question about where the Mormons were holding their worship services, I cannot be sure, but he raised the broom above his head and chased me from the grounds.

I decided it was probably safer not to antagonize anyone else that morning and so commenced to walk toward Town Centre. I could not describe the route I followed, but I know I had walked approximately twenty-five minutes when, turning a corner, I saw a parked van with the name *Rayarts* displayed on the side panel. I recognized it as belonging to Brother Arthur Gibbs, a district councilman who used the van in his TV and audio retail and repair business. Adjacent to the vehicle was a community hall where I discovered the Saints of the Colchester Branch had gathered for their worship services. Thinking of how I came to find the place, I am reminded of the Lord's promise that as a result of faithful adherence to the baptismal covenant, "He [will] pour out His spirit more abundantly upon [us]" (Mosiah 18:10). I acknowledge this to be the means by which I was led to the meeting place and testify that making and keeping covenants will bring an abundance of blessings to enrich our lives and enlarge our understanding of eternal truths.

As I entered the room where the MIA leaders were gathered, President Wheeler arose from his seat to commence the meeting. This was a significant improvement compared to my previous arrival at the conclusion of the meeting.

Following words of welcome and introduction, President Wheeler announced that we would be privileged to receive a forty-five-minute presentation on the age-group program from the newly called counselor in the district MIA presidency, Brother Kenneth Johnson.

At the time of my call I had been given some manuals to

study, but I had had little time to absorb their contents, and I had not been given a specific assignment for this meeting. Rising to my feet, I expressed my feelings and personal testimony, concluding in about two minutes. President Wheeler was very gracious in expressing his appreciation for my contribution, but I was, of course, embarrassed by my lack of preparation. I learned so much from each of these experiences and determined not to repeat my mistakes. I was beginning to realize that our happiness is not dictated by our circumstances; rather, it is one of the fruits of our service.

## ATHLETIC ENDEAVORS

Constancy and persistence are essential qualities in the pursuit of personal progress and individual achievements. I had always derived deep satisfaction and a high degree of enjoyment from participating in athletic events. Two contrasting experiences have become memorable and edifying when examined in the glow of gospel light.

We were preparing for athletic competition in my first year at college. I had been selected to represent Ramage House in several events, including the long jump. In the practice heats, I was leading with a jump of thirteen feet until a fellow named Snodgrass representing White House jumped sixteen feet. As we prepared for our final attempts, Snodgrass was confident that he would be the champion. His supremacy seemed obvious to me as well, since it didn't seem likely that I would be able to increase my leap by an additional three feet. However, I determined to do the best I could.

In his three final attempts, Snodgrass was unable to pace his run to the long-jump pit, and each time he was adjudged to have stepped over the marker board, which resulted in his disqualification. I managed a jump of nearly thirteen feet four inches and won the event, receiving a medal for my achievement. My achievement was a lesson in constancy and persistence. In life, we are not competing with others in principles of personal progress; we should only be trying to be our best selves.

My sporting interest included running the 400-meter race. Having finished first in the preliminary competition, I was nominated to participate in the local school's championship. In the heat that I was designated to run, I drew the outside lane assignment on an oval track. Since I would have farther to run on the outside lane, I was given a starting position well ahead of the other competitors and from which I could not see them. For some reason I had never run from this staggered alignment before, and it seemed strange to be starting from a position that appeared to be so far in advance of my fellow athletes.

Not being able to see where the other competitors were and not wishing to be overtaken over the final stretch of the race, I set off at a good pace when the starter's gun sounded. I finished first, some distance ahead of the other runners and equaling the record for the race in that category. But fifteen minutes later, when the names of competitors were announced to participate in the final heat, I was too exhausted to make my way to the starting line. I was unwise to have exerted all my energy in the preliminary heat.

In Mosiah 4:27 we read, "And see that all these things are done in wisdom and order; for it is not requisite that a man should run faster than he has strength. And again, it is expedient that he should be diligent, that thereby he might win the prize; therefore, all things must be done in order."

## COVENANTS, CALLINGS, AND SACRIFICE

When we are constant in keeping covenants, we develop a wisdom that will safeguard us from the condition frequently referred to as burnout. I believe these possibilities are alluded to in D&C 84:33, wherein the Lord speaks to those who faithfully adhere to the oath and covenant of the priesthood: "For whoso is faithful unto the obtaining these two priesthoods of which I have spoken, and the magnifying their calling, are sanctified by the Spirit unto the renewing of their bodies."

D&C 97:8 makes reference to those honest in heart who are "willing to observe their covenants by sacrifice." Discovering the relationship between covenants and callings was an important step in my conversion. I came to understand that our response to—and fulfillment of—the callings we receive is a reflection of our dedication to the covenants we have made. The covenants precede the callings and continue following a release. A call to serve is an assignment under the covenant.

Covenants also provide a compass by which we can set the course of our lives. Initially it may be difficult to appreciate the benefits that result when we voluntarily bind ourselves to act by covenant. In his memorable sermon, King Benjamin taught this principle: "And now, because of the covenant which ye have made ye shall be called the children of Christ, his sons, and his daughters; for behold, this day he hath spiritually begotten you; for ye say that your hearts are changed through faith on his name; therefore, ye are born of him and have become his sons and his daughters. And under this head ye are made free, and there is no other head whereby ye can be made free. There is no other name given whereby salvation cometh; therefore, I would that ye should take upon you the name of Christ, all you that have entered into the covenant with God that ye should be obedient unto the end of your lives" (Mosiah 5:7-8).

I believe that as we develop a deeper understanding of the gospel, we are impressed to strengthen our devotion to our covenants.

## A DEEPER DETERMINATION

September 30, 1966, was a special day for our family and particularly significant for me. It was the day our son was born.

We didn't contemplate any unusual difficulty with his birth, so we made arrangements for a midwife to deliver him in the bedroom of our home. Pamela's mother, Evelyn Wilson, ever eager to help, was there to assist. The labor turned out to be extended, and the anticipated invitation to greet the baby was slow in coming. After finally hearing the familiar cry of a newborn baby, I listened to the sound of anxious voices and footsteps as those attending Pamela descended and ascended the stairs. A doctor arrived and spent some time with Pamela. Banished from the delivery, I had not been permitted to enter the room, and my inquiries for information had been greeted with words intended to reassure me that all was well.

The doctor eventually came into the room where I was anxiously waiting and announced that all was not well with the baby, that there were some serious birth defects and that he would have to be transferred to the hospital. The man was not Pamela's regular physician and so, after phoning for an ambulance, he left the midwife to care for our son.

Kevin looked so healthy, it was hard to imagine that all was not well. Following a priesthood blessing, he was taken to the hospital by ambulance. When Pamela's regular doctor arrived, she announced that Kevin would likely not survive.

Devastated by that disclosure, I retired later that morning to a secluded area in our home and prayed in a way that I had never done before. In effect, I said, "Heavenly Father, if thou wilt spare our son, I will give my life in service to thee." It was as if all the covenants I had previously entered into had been made almost perfunctorily. Those covenants then became much more binding for me. Yes, I had been faithful, serving in the Church happily without reservation, but I was then prepared to submit my will *entirely* to the Lord's will. It was a defining moment—a covenantal conversion. Through divine intervention and medical attention, Kevin did survive and has since grown to manhood.

## THE HOMECOMING

As we cleave unto our covenants, we discover the real treasures of life and of eternity. All that is precious to me is linked to the covenants I have made. An experience I had while traveling to general conference as a counselor in a stake presidency in the mid 1970s provided a vivid insight into what results from constancy in keeping covenants.

I had traveled from London on a transatlantic flight to St. Louis, where we connected with a flight to Salt Lake City. Some young men returning from full-time missionary service boarded the flight in St. Louis on the last leg of their journey home. They excitedly related to me some of their missionary experiences. They were at the in-between stage—eager to be reunited with their families but still clinging to the people and memories of their missions.

The Salt Lake City airport was not at that time fully equipped with jetways to facilitate deplaning, and portable steps were rolled to the aircraft door for this purpose. As I walked across the tarmac toward the terminal building, one of the young missionaries walked ahead of me. Before we reached the entrance to the terminal building, a little girl about two years of age ran toward him with outstretched arms, and in a leaping motion clasped his legs around the thighs and planted her feet on his to be carried, somewhat awkwardly by the missionary, into the building. Once inside, the elder was encircled in the loving arms of family and friends.

This scene provided a perfect picture of how covenants can link families through the veil of death. I concluded that the little girl who was a central figure in this drama was the missionary's sister and would not have been old enough to have remembered her brother prior to his mission. Her love for him would have developed as she heard her parents and family members speak of her absent brother. I thought of the similarity of these circumstances to those that will exist at the close of our mortal mission as long as we are bonded together by covenant.

Consider the Lord's counsel to Emma Smith: "Wherefore; lift up thy heart and rejoice, and cleave unto the covenants which thou hast made" (D&C 25:3). These words reflect my feelings and express my desire. Whether it be in the warmth of the family circle or the joy of Church service, my greatest aspiration is to cleave unto my covenants.

# A PATRIARCHAL
# BLESSING

## RECEIVING AND INTERPRETING

On May 19, 1963, several branch members and I traveled from Norwich to Leicester to receive our patriarchal blessings from Oliver Storer, the patriarch in the nearest stake to where we lived. Following a brief introductory discussion, Brother Storer placed his hands on my head and pronounced my blessing. Recognizing the personal nature and sacredness of a patriarchal blessing, I share only the following sentence from mine: "Now you shall be engaged in a good work, even to instructing in the priesthood, even to a high and holy calling within that priesthood as you progress and develop, and the Spirit of the Lord shall be upon you."

I considered my calling to serve as a counselor in the branch presidency a fulfillment of that promise. Seven years later, when I was called as a counselor in a district presidency, I saw that to be the position referred to. Twelve months later, in June 1971, the district was organized as a stake, and I was called to serve as a counselor in the stake presidency. Then, in January 1977, President Dennis Reeves, who was serving as stake president, received a letter from the First Presidency announcing that the stake presidency would be reorganized at the conference to be held February 19–20. It had been a great privilege and wonderful opportunity to serve with President Reeves, and I had learned much through my association with the other members of the stake presidency, high council, and with other stake and ward leaders.

## CALLED TO SERVE AS A STAKE PRESIDENT

Interviews to find who the Lord had prepared to serve as stake president were scheduled for Friday evening, February 18. I drove the forty-three miles from Norwich to the stake center in Ipswich accompanied by three other brethren who had been invited for interviews. As second counselor in the stake presidency, I was the third person to be interviewed. It was an overwhelming experience to be in the presence of an Apostle, a member of the Seventy, and a regional representative. The member of the Twelve thanked me for serving, asked me for my observations, and then excused me with the words, "You can go home now." I left the office and announced to my traveling companions that I had been instructed to return home but reassured them that I would not leave until after they had been interviewed.

Approximately twenty minutes later, President Reeves approached to advise me that the brethren conducting the interviews wished to speak with me again. This time the Apostle posed some questions relating to my feelings about being released, including, "How would you feel about being a home teacher?" I responded that I enjoyed the opportunities associated with home teaching and that I would probably have more time to dedicate to the families entrusted to my care following my release. I was again excused and told that I was free to go home.

Another twenty to twenty-five minutes passed, and I was still waiting for one of my fellow travelers. President Reeves approached me once more, indicating that I had been requested to return to the stake president's office where the interviews were being conducted. There was a different atmosphere in the room. The member of the Twelve asked some searching questions and then called me to serve as stake president. It was a humbling experience; one that I had not anticipated. I recall thinking that this must surely be the calling referred to in my patriarchal blessing. I maintained my composure only by reminding myself that I had served as a counselor and so had a good insight into what was required of a stake president.

Reflecting on my new calling, the next day I attended the Saturday afternoon priesthood leadership meeting and the evening adult meeting. My mind was not focused on the meeting as it should have been. The events that followed left an indelible impression upon my mind and had a profound influence on my life.

## A REFINING EXPERIENCE

The visiting member of the Twelve was addressing the congregation of approximately three hundred. My mind was partially in the meeting and partially occupied thinking about the responsibility that was to distill upon me. My attention was captured when I realized that the speaker was no longer addressing the congregation but was looking at me. He asked, "Do you remember what the theme of this meeting was one year ago?"

All eyes were upon me, and the congregation waited in silence for my response.

"Keeping personal and family histories," I replied. I felt a brief sense of achievement, but the questioning had not concluded.

"Have you written yours?"

"No," I said simply, having nowhere to hide.

"Why not?"

At this point, the speaker continued his message to the congregation.

I thought it quite remarkable that the following day, when I was sustained as stake president, even those who had attended the Saturday evening meeting raised their hands in support, notwithstanding my confessed weakness.

I spent the remainder of that day, even awakening during the night, considering what I should do as stake president. Monday morning I did not feel well. Not only did I have a feeling of nausea, but I experienced an oppressive overshadowing cloud of darkness. I decided that this would not persist and, without mentioning how I felt, went to my business office as usual. The feeling of depression remained with me until Thursday morning, when I concluded that my sickness was related to my call to serve as stake president. I had struggled to determine what I should focus on in this significant assignment but had come to no clear decision. My initial response was to phone the Apostle who had called me to tell him that I was not qualified for such a calling. With those thoughts in mind, I went so far as to calculate the time difference between England and Salt Lake City.

In the midst of this dilemma, I heard the voice of the Spirit in my mind communicate this message: "You don't have to lead this stake, I will. Just follow me."

It was as if a light had been switched on and heavy weights lifted from my body. My feelings were transformed from doubt and despair to jubilation. In the turmoil associated with such a traumatic experience, I had overlooked the most important aspect of Church leadership responsibility—the Spirit.

I reflected on what had happened just prior to my being set apart as the president of the stake. As we assembled after the conference meetings for this purpose, I sat in a chair next to President Reeves, a position I had become comfortable in for almost seven years. The Apostle asked why I had chosen that particular place to sit. Impetuously, I responded, "I know where the revelation comes from." It was not a wise response and I knew it.

"Not anymore" he replied. "If any revelation comes for this stake while you serve as the president, it will come through you."

## REFLECTIONS AND REVELATION

Yes, the most important resource available to a leader in the Church is access to revelation through the companionship of the Spirit. With this realization I would have been comfortable serving as a stake president for twenty, thirty, forty, or fifty years. It is exhilarating to have one's mind renewed from such a source, recognizing that this enhanced capacity results from the Lord's recognition of the needs of an enlarged circle of people who depend on you for counsel and direction. The wise leader does not seek personal acclaim but does all things with an eye single to the glory of God, seeking "earnestly the best gifts, always remembering for what they are given . . . that all may be profited thereby" (D&C 46:8, 12).

Following my release as stake president in May 1986, I served as the stake institute teacher and ward gospel doctrine teacher. I was later called to serve as a counselor in a bishopric, and in March 1987 as a regional representative. This extended my sphere of involvement and exposure to Church leaders and procedures and brought me greater insights and an expanded vision of the workings of the Church. The assignment to serve as regional representative included an opportunity to work on the committee planning the celebration of the 150th anniversary of missionaries arriving in the British Isles to proclaim the restoration of the gospel. Twenty-five years earlier when I received my patriarchal blessing, I had no comprehension that such opportunities to serve would even exist.

## A CALL TO THE QUORUMS OF THE SEVENTY

Another memorable landmark in my life began with a telephone call I received at 9:00 P.M. on March 23, 1990. Pamela was serving as the ward Young Women president, and that evening she had attended an activity. I had arranged to pick her up from the chapel at 9:15 P.M. and was just leaving our home when the familiar sound of the telephone ring pierced the air. I literally had my hand on the door handle but walked back to where the telephone was located to inquire who was calling.

The man gave me his name and indicated that he was a secretary to the First Presidency. He asked if I was Elder Kenneth Johnson, the regional representative.

I responded affirmatively, and he advised me that President Gordon B. Hinckley (then serving as first counselor in the First Presidency) wished to speak with me. Following a short pause, President Hinckley asked if I was well, but I sensed that this was not a casual inquiry. I confirmed that I was. He posed further questions, then asked if I was planning to attend the upcoming general conference. I replied that I was, in the capacity of a regional representative. He then asked if Pamela would be accompanying me, and when I responded that she would not, President Hinckley said, "Why don't you bring her with you?" I agreed that I would, and he concluded the conversation by saying, "I would like to meet with you on Thursday afternoon prior to conference. Phone my secretary when you arrive in town, and she will finalize the arrangements."

Replacing the phone handset in its resting place, I quickly left to pick up Pamela as arranged. When I arrived at the chapel, the activity had concluded, and the leaders were clearing away the materials used. Approaching Pamela, I greeted her, then said I had something I needed to discuss with her. She asked if it was important or if it could wait until after she had completed the task at hand. I suggested that she might feel that it was important, and, sensing that the subject was confidential, she excused herself to the others, and we walked from the classroom into the corridor.

Without prolonged explanation, I said, "You are going to general conference."

"I thought we had decided that I would not travel with you on this occasion," she replied.

"President Hinckley has invited you," I said.

"Oh, then I am going to general conference!"

I shared with her what President Hinckley had said on the telephone, and she joined me in wondering why he would want to meet with both of us. Though it had been three years since the sesquicentennial celebration of the introduction of the gospel in the British Isles, we wondered if there might not be some continuing matters to be handled. Mission presidents who were to commence their missions in July of that year had already been contacted and called, so I eliminated that as a consideration; in fact, I did not really consider that to even be a possibility. We eventually settled our minds that it probably had something to do with my current assignment.

On the Tuesday morning before general conference, Pamela and I boarded the flight from London to the United States, traveling first to Los Angeles, where we met with Conrad Burgoyne and the British ambassador to address some visa concerns. We arrived in Salt Lake City on Wednesday afternoon, and after checking into a hotel, I telephoned President Hinckley's office and booked an appointment for 2:30 P.M. on Thursday. Anxious not to be late, Pamela and I arrived early at the reception area of the Church Administration Building. Just prior to 2:30 P.M., a female secretary came to the area and invited me to accompany her to President Hinckley's office.

He greeted me warmly, and we spoke for a time of his experiences in England and also discussed my own background. After a very pleasant conversation, President Hinckley asked if Pamela had accompanied me. I confirmed that she had and was waiting in the reception area. He requested that I invite her into his office.

I returned to where she was waiting and invited her in. Anxious to know what had transpired, she asked me in a hushed voice, "What is it?" I had to tell her I didn't know.

We entered the office, and President Hinckley greeted Pamela. He then commenced to ask her questions about us and then more specifically about my qualities as a husband and father. This exchange continued for a while, and I observed their interaction with great interest. Eventually, President Hinckley turned his attention to me, and I realized I was being interviewed. When President Hinckley extended the call on behalf of the Lord for me to serve as a General Authority, I was absolutely stunned. It was as if I had fallen into a deep pit and was trying to grasp hold of something to stop my fall. I had never even contemplated such a possibility.

This marked another phase of refinement in my life. I had already covenanted to serve the Lord when I was baptized, ordained to the Melchizedek Priesthood, and endowed in the House of the Lord. Now I was being asked to demonstrate my further allegiance to the gospel cause and to the covenants I had made.

My memory is vague concerning the events that followed, but I recall that after leaving the Church Administration Building and while walking through the foyer of the Church Office Building, I encountered the Apostle who had called me to serve as a stake president. He asked if I had been interviewed. I was still in a state of shock, and after responding affirmatively, I proceeded to ask him a series of questions relative to what I should do. His response was profound and has had a continuing relevance in my life.

Raising his right hand to waist level with his fingers outstretched, he positioned his index finger approximately one inch above his thumb, indicating that only a small portion of what I needed to fulfill my new calling would come from down here on earth. Emphasizing the necessity of seeking and receiving inspiration in order to fulfill the responsibility that had been entrusted to me, he indicated that the rest of the help I needed would come from heaven,

## CALLINGS AND COVENANTS

A covenant is an agreement between God and man. After I became a member of the Church, through the covenant of baptism, I was given an opportunity to serve through the various callings that came to me. In the course of that service I came to understand that every calling is an assignment under our covenants. However, whereas callings last only for a season, covenants are in force forever, providing we are true and faithful. My covenants, therefore, are more sacred to me than my callings. That is not to suggest that I lack devotion in fulfilling my Church assignments, but I have a conviction that it is by keeping our covenants that we will reach our full eternal potential.

All that is most precious to me is associated with the covenants I have made. Among those precious things are:
- My love for and affinity with my Heavenly Father
- My gratitude to Jesus Christ and my testimony of his divinity as the Son of God, our Savior and Redeemer
- The gift of the Holy Ghost

- My temple covenants and the eternal nature of my family relationships
- My loyalty and allegiance to the Church and my commitment to serve faithfully in my priesthood assignments

Focusing on the family does not restrict our availability for Church service. The author of our call to serve will magnify our capacity to effectively take care of both responsibilities if we are willing participants. The lessons I have learned and the refinement I have experienced through Church service, along with the accompanying direction from the Holy Spirit have greatly enhanced my abilities as a husband and father.

# "MY JOY IS MORE FULL"

## HELPING OTHERS SUCCEED

Describing his feelings about his ministry, Alma the Younger declared: "I do not joy in my own success alone, but my joy is more full because of the success of my brethren" (Alma 29:14). In this statement, Alma points out one of the sources of real happiness—finding joy in the accomplishments of others.

What a wonderful thing it is to rejoice in the success of family members, Church associates, fellow employees, and neighbors. When I ponder this principle, I think of my wife, Pamela, who has been for me one of the greatest practitioners of this art. An experience we had in our family illustrates what I mean.

## OPTIMISM AND DETERMINATION

As I have noted, our son, Kevin, was born with some very severe physical problems. When he was six years old, he underwent surgery to correct the alignment of his hips. It was an extensive operation, and he was required afterward to spend many weeks confined in the hospital.

During the days following the surgery, Kevin was kept lying on his back with his feet suspended above his bed in a gallows-like apparatus that held his legs and hips positioned at an awkward, forty-five-degree angle. Eventually, a stack of pillows was used to support his legs, and as the healing progressed, pillows were gradually removed until he was lowered into a normal reclining position on the bed.

When the doctor determined it was safe, Kevin was finally permitted to get out of bed. His legs were so weak, though, that he couldn't stand without assistance. Had Pamela and two nurses not been there to support him, he would have collapsed. But rather than become alarmed and complain, Kevin began to giggle. That was the beginning of a long period of recovery, which required extensive physical therapy in the hospital and continuing rehabilitation at home.

Kevin was eager to return to school. So within a week of his release from the hospital, Pamela and I agreed that he could resume his studies, as long as he would take care to restrict his activities according to his limitations. To conserve his strength and energy, Pamela would either carry him piggy back or push him on a foot-propelled scooter to and from school.

Approximately fourteen days after Kevin returned to school, Pamela received a telephone call from his teacher, a Mrs. Barber, who caused us some concern by saying, "We are worried about Kevin."

Pamela responded anxiously, "Is he ill?"

"Oh, no" she replied. "He is doing very well. It is what he is proposing to do that concerns us."

She explained that the school was going to hold a sports activity in three weeks. She wanted to know what to do because, she said, "Kevin has entered every race."

Pamela paused and then said, "Thank you for calling. His father and I will speak with him about it this evening."

When Pamela picked him up from school that day, she asked him if he thought he was physically strong enough to participate in school sports. He nonchalantly responded, "I will be when the sports event is held in three weeks. That's a long time ahead."

## THE DAY OF THE RACE

When I returned from the office that day, Pamela told me about Mrs. Barber's call, and the two of us discussed with Kevin our reservations about his participating in sports events so soon after having undergone such extensive surgery. He expressed his confidence that there was nothing to be concerned about and that he would be strong enough to run the races.

The three weeks passed quickly, and it was soon the morning of the school sports event. Pamela had prepared Kevin's white T-shirt, shorts, socks, and running shoes. Dressed in this attire, his face radiated excitement and self-confidence. After arriving at the school sports field, Pamela and I took our places with the other parents while Kevin joined his fellow competitors.

When Kevin and his class members lined up for their first race, he had a look of intense determination on his face. At the sound of a teacher's whistle, the race began, and the children headed toward the tape that marked the finishing line. From the perspective of these young competitors, this could have been a race in the Olympic games held in a giant stadium with a large crowd urging them on. Though he gave it all he had, Kevin was left behind the surging pack of runners and finished last by some considerable distance. It was painful to watch, but we were proud that he kept running until he had completed the course.

As he returned to the waiting area with his fellow runners, he walked past us and shrugged his shoulders as if to communicate, "I don't know what happened in that race, but you wait until the next one."

The runners lined up for the second race in their age group. The sound of the teacher's whistle once again pierced the air, and the race was on. The results were the same: Kevin was left behind the others, and once again finished last. This time as he passed us on the way to the waiting area, we could tell he was beginning to feel a little despondent over his lack of success. The third race added further to the realization that he had not yet regained his physical strength to the degree he had believed.

All parents know there are moments when they feel compelled to rush from the sidelines and rescue their children rather than watch them continue to struggle against overwhelming difficulties. That was my feeling on that occasion. I wanted to pick Kevin up and run with him to win the race, but I realized that would not have helped him overcome his growing feelings of inadequacy.

## "I TRIED"

While witnessing this and struggling to know what I should do, Pamela's voice jolted my mind back to reality, particularly since I thought I had misheard her. Then she said again, "Let's go home."

I was shocked. It didn't seem possible that she was proposing that we desert our son at one of the most difficult moments of his young life. The look on my face must have communicated my thoughts as Pamela continued, "It won't take us long."

Recognizing that Pamela had been prompted what to do, we ran to our parked car and drove to our home. As instructed, I stayed in the car parked in the driveway with the engine running while Pamela dashed into the house and returned after a short time clutching a roll of red crepe paper, a pair of scissors, a piece of poster board, a safety pin, and a black marker pen. While I drove us back to the school grounds, Pamela quickly fashioned a round rosette out of the poster board and decorated it with ribbons of crepe paper. Using the pen, she wrote on the makeshift medallion the words "I TRIED."

It was obvious when we returned to the school grounds that Kevin had failed in another race and was even more despondent. The winners of the races had been awarded ribbons—a red ribbon for first place, yellow for second, and blue for third. Many of the children were proudly displaying these indicators of their achievements. Pamela beckoned for Kevin to come to where we were standing and using the safety pin, attached the medallion she had made to his white T-shirt. When she asked him if he could read what was written on the medallion, Kevin beamed as he read aloud, "I TRIED." Somehow in that moment all the hurt and pain of not being able to run with the rest of his classmates was swept away. A mother's inspiration had once more been sufficient to the needs of her child.

Having enjoyed many such moments, when spiritual promptings have come to my companion, I have often read with a deep sense of appreciation these words from the scriptures: "[God] imparteth his word by angels unto men, yea, not only men, but *women* also" (Alma 32:23; emphasis added).

## BLIND BARTIMAEUS

It is natural to want to see our loved ones succeed. When they face difficulties and obstacles, we spontaneously reach out to them with words of encouragement and expressions of support. To do so in behalf of those with whom we do not have this affinity takes a greater depth of character. In this matter of demonstrating love, the Savior is our great exemplar. I have been particularly impressed by the account of Jesus' encounter with a man named Bartimaeus.

Bartimaeus was a blind man who sat begging by the highway on the outskirts of Jericho. When he heard the sound of a

crowd of people approaching and learned that they were following Jesus of Nazareth, he began to cry out, saying, "Jesus,
thou son of David, have mercy on me" (Mark 10:47). Many
charged the man that he should hold his peace; but he cried
the more. Above the sound of the crowd, Jesus heard the voice
of Bartimaeus and sent for him.

The account continues: "And they call the blind man, saying unto him, Be of good comfort, rise; he calleth thee. And he,
casting away his garment, rose, and came unto Jesus. And Jesus
answered and said unto him, What wilt thou that I should do
unto thee? The blind man said unto him, Lord, that I might
receive my sight. And Jesus said unto him, Go thy way; thy
faith hath made thee whole." The scriptures record that
Bartimaeus immediately "received his sight, and followed Jesus
in the way" (Mark 10:49–52).

One cannot overestimate the significance of this miracle,
but it is equally impressive that Jesus was aware of and sensi-
tive to Bartimaeus. The Savior's ability to reach out to the
otherwise unnoticed is a powerful example for us. Could it
be that we are distracted from those in need by other less-
important matters? Robert Browning's reminder to "look outside yourself with love, and you will have joy" has real merit.

## THE VICTORY

The years rolled by and Kevin was not only able to walk
and run but became an outstanding athlete. He particularly
loved to play football (soccer), and when he was fourteen years
old, he and other members of the Norwich Ward competed in
a Church regional "five-a-side" tournament for boys ages fourteen to seventeen. The Norwich team had won each of its qualifying games and was to play in the tournament final, which
was scheduled for a 6:30 start on a Saturday morning. The
game was to be played at a facility called Pontins Holiday
Camp at Pakefield on the east coast of England near Lowestoft

in Suffolk. Pamela and I stayed overnight at the site, and the next morning walked over to the pitch where the game would be played. As might be expected, few spectators had shown up for the early game.

When the players of the opposing team appeared, they were obviously in the upper portion of that age group and much taller on average than the team from Norwich. This had an adverse psychological effect on Kevin and his teammates, and some of them expressed the view that there was no way they could win the game. Ever optimistic, I interjected some words of encouragement, hoping to change their attitude. But when the game commenced, it was obvious that they felt winning was an insurmountable task. They soon conceded one goal and then another, and it looked as though the two-goal deficit would continue to mount to four, five, or more.

I began to run up and down the sideline, shouting words of encouragement. Incredibly, our Norwich boys scored one goal and then a second. At halftime, the score was tied at two goals each. During the halftime period, I expressed additional words of encouragement and continued to run the line during the second half, shouting words of support. The Norwich team scored a third goal and then a fourth goal while holding their opponents scoreless, winning the competition by four goals to two.

Our son and I have often reflected on that day, reliving the joy of the experience together. He scored three of the four goals and speaks of the thrill that he and his teammates enjoyed in such a remarkable achievement, and of the difference my words of encouragement had made. In light of the physical disadvantages Kevin had overcome, it was an indescribable thrill to witness his success. I am confident that he has never fully comprehended my joy at witnessing such a moment in his life.

Truly "my joy [was] more full because of the success of [one of] my brethren."

## DEREK REDMAN—A BRITISH ATHLETE

I have learned many lessons from participating in and by being a spectator of sporting activities. The 1992 Olympics produced one of those memorable lessons. My interest was captured that year by the achievements of Derek Redman, a British 400-meter runner. The media had reported that this Olympic hopeful had sustained a career-threatening injury and would not be able to run at an international level again. But over a long period of time, he trained, endured prolonged, painful physical therapy, and gradually worked his way back to fitness, winning a place on the British 1992 Olympic squad. I admired his courage and respected him for overcoming a seemingly insurmountable obstacle in his life. I made it a point to watch the televised races in which he competed.

In his first heat, Derek performed effortlessly and crossed the finish line in first place. In the second heat he repeated his accomplishment. The British media were now contemplating the possibility of Derek winning a medal in this event.

In the semifinal race, Derek set off as he had in the previous races, running effortlessly in a demonstration of his characteristic grace and power. He was going well when almost as if he had be hit by a bullet from a gun, he pulled up lame, clasping his leg with his hand. Hobbling, he struggled on, trying to move forward. Even though Derek was not impeding the other runners, stewards moved quickly to escort him from the track. Their intent was obviously to assist him, but he pushed them away.

Then the camera focused on a man moving through the crowd down to the barricade at the edge of the track. The man climbed over the barricade and jogged to where Derek was moving forward with great difficulty. As the spectator approached, Derek seemed to be preparing to reject any assistance as he had previously. The camera picked up the lip movements of the spectator as he approached the flagging athlete, and Derek finally stretched out his arm, accepting assistance. Together, the two men completed the course and crossed the finish line.

The man who had come out of the crowd of spectators was Derek's father. I had some sense of how he felt. He knew that Derek would never compete in the Olympics again and that his son's desire would be to cross the finish line in this, his last race.

## STRENGTHEN THY BRETHREN

Such experiences awaken within me a deep appreciation for the opportunities we have to help one another as children of God and as Latter-day Saints. The scriptures enjoin us to do so: "Therefore, strengthen your brethren in all your conversation, in all your prayers, in all your exhortations, and in all your doings." The promise in return for obedience to this commandment is "I [will be] with you to bless you and deliver you forever" (D&C 108:7-8). Following this practice would preclude our ever having to attend an uninteresting meeting or class. Our desire would be to help every speaker and teacher succeed in their assignment by lending our faith, prayers, and active participation when appropriate.

In my early stages of learning the gospel, I was dependent upon the testimony and teaching of others. Now when I attend a meeting or am present in class, I am not restricted to learning only from the speaker or teacher, though their words often prompt deeper consideration. I have a sufficient fabric of faith to be able to explore in my mind and ponder in my heart things beyond what the speaker or teacher might share. Therefore I do not hold the person presenting the message responsible for the quality of the meeting or lesson. What I get out of the message depends in large part on me and my capacity to commune with the Spirit.

The procedure of raising our hands to sustain those called to serve in the Church is related to this principle. None of us are without some degree of imperfection, but we can still qualify ourselves to respond to a call from the Lord. With divine guidance and the sustaining support of the Saints, ordinary people can achieve extraordinary things as they become instruments in the hands of the Lord.

When Church leaders follow the Savior's pattern of leadership, as demonstrated in his earthly ministry and prescribed in the scriptures, the Lord's work moves forward in a wonderful way—blessing lives, building faith, and strengthening testimonies: "Wherefore, be faithful; stand in the office which I have appointed unto you; succor the weak, lift up the hands which hang down, and strengthen the feeble knees." The scripture continues with a description of the blessings that flow from the application of these principles and refers to the reward of a "crown of immortality, and eternal life" (D&C 81:5-6). That is what our Heavenly Father desires for each of us. His joy is derived from our success. I believe that true success is to stand with confidence in the presence of God. But I do not joy in my own success alone, for my joy is more full because of the success of my brethren and sisters.

# PART THREE

*Beliefs Confirmed*

# "TREASURE UP IN YOUR MINDS CONTINUALLY THE WORDS OF LIFE"

Our communities are increasingly decorated with traffic signals, road markings, and warning signs, many of which are easily recognizable and clearly understood. Others can sometimes create confusion and seem to be unnecessary or redundant.

## BEWARE—LOW-FLYING AIRCRAFT

Some years ago, Ken Groom and I had a home teaching assignment to a family by the name of Houghton. Brother Houghton was a pilot in the United States Air Force, and in an exchange arrangement between Great Britain and the Allied Forces, he was stationed at the Royal Air Force Base in Coltishall, Norfolk, England. On the perimeter road approaching their residence on the air base, a sign displayed the warning: "Beware—Low-Flying Aircraft."

Each time I passed the warning, I smiled, visualizing myself having to maneuver my vehicle to avoid a fleet of low-flying fighter jets. I could not imagine why it had been erected there.

My illusion was shattered one evening as Brother Groom and I were driving past the sign as a jet fighter was descending toward us in a landing approach. The narrow road upon which we were traveling had no protective rail on one side, and the adjoining land fell away sharply into a ditch. Opposite was the fencing that secured the airfield. As the plane roared immediately overhead, the deafening noise left me momentarily disoriented. I struggled to control the car and feared for a moment that we might veer off the road into the ditch. I was surprised to be unable to determine where the aircraft was in relation to my vehicle. The whole experience probably lasted for only a few moments but was dramatically exaggerated by the intensity of the noise and proximity of the plane. As I watched the aircraft land safely on the runway, I reflected on how grateful I was that someone had been wise enough to erect a sign warning of "low-flying aircraft." I then more fully understood its significance.

So often in our lives, particularly during our teenage years, we do not appreciate or recognize the value of counsel and advice we receive from parents, teachers, and Church leaders. We only understand and feel grateful after we have had an experience that clarifies the wisdom behind the words of caution given and the restrictions imposed.

## CHARACTER DEVELOPMENT

The Lord has counseled us to "treasure up in [our] minds continually the words of life." We are promised that if we will do so, the things we have pondered will be brought to our remembrance when needed (see D&C 84:85). An experience I had while attending college would have provided a wonderful opportunity to learn this lesson and avoid future difficulties had I understood then the principle of treasuring up.

I was enthusiastically involved in soccer, cricket, and other athletic programs but was not as interested in playing rugby, which was a college curriculum requirement. The sports teacher, Mr. Jack Adams, had been a physical fitness instructor in the British Army and certainly knew how to command respect. I recall attending a physical education class under his direction in the college gymnasium, wearing the mandated attire of white T-shirt, white shorts, white socks, and white sports shoes, which on this occasion were blemished by a black mark on the toe cap. By way of penance, Mr. Adams instructed me to remove my socks and shoes and to run barefoot four laps around the gravel path adjacent to the gymnasium. His method of teaching was very effective, and I never again attended a class of his wearing anything but immaculately clean attire.

Motivated ostensibly by a desire to develop character in the young men who passed through his "care," Mr. Adams developed a number of activities that we students considered to be torturous.

## THE COLLEGE RUGBY TEAM

I remember attending a rugby training session when the ground was frozen so hard the groundsmen had declared it unfit for play. Mr. Adams felt it was important not to miss a training session, and notwithstanding the frozen field ushered us out onto the grassy area adjacent to the rugby pitch to practice our skills. One of the drills he had devised was tackling practice. He divided the students into two groups. The first group formed a line about thirty yards from the second group. Students in the second group were instructed to stand with their backs toward the first group. At Mr. Adams' command, members of the first group ran toward and tackled from behind someone in the second group. Those being tackled pitched forward onto the frozen surface with painful results. After several attempts, Mr. Adams would reverse the roles of the two lines so that all could practice tackling techniques.

Needless to say, I did not enjoy this activity and was not attentive to the instructions given.

The following week Mr. Adams approached me and, to my amazement, informed me that I had been selected to be a member of the college rugby team and would play the fullback position. He commented that my ability to handle, kick, and pass the ball accurately had convinced him of my value to the team. He also said an intersquad game was scheduled as a final practice before league play began.

From my perspective, the intersquad game progressed well for the first fifteen minutes. I had gathered the ball and either passed or kicked for touch successfully. But then there was a scrimmage close to the halfway line, and out of a ruck of players, a student named Riley emerged clutching the ball to his chest. He weighed 225 pounds, and the ground appeared to shake as he ran toward me. I then realized the only obstacle between him and the goal line was my 112-pound frame.

Riley's red hair was blowing in the wind like flames from a fire as he thundered toward me. In a desperate attempt to stop him, I threw myself toward him but only succeeded in bouncing painfully off his torso. I hit the ground clasping his ankle and was dragged over the line as Riley completed the touchdown. It occurred to me that if only I had listened and observed Mr. Adams' instructions that frosty morning, I perhaps would have known better how to arrest the progress of a moving mass more than twice my body weight. As a result of my failure, I was relieved of my duties as fullback and transferred to the position of wing forward. I learned from my experience that we can underestimate the value of instructions that do not appear to have immediate relevance.

Great benefits and wonderful blessings are associated with treasuring up in one's mind good thoughts, wise counsel, and inspired instruction. On numerous occasions and in a variety of circumstances useful things have been brought to my remembrance. I had one such experience while learning to drive a car.

## REFINING OUR THOUGHTS

Mr. Westhorpe, my driving instructor, rehearsed many scenarios that I did not encounter while under his tutelage, but motivated by a desire to be a competent driver and to obtain a driving license, I listened intently. Some ten years later, while serving as a counselor in a stake presidency, I set out early one Sunday morning to attend the Thetford Ward meetings twenty-eight miles from my home. It was a frosty winter's day, and stretches of the road were marked with signs warning of the possibility of black ice. Aware of the danger, I drove cautiously.

After passing through the small community of Hethersett, I overtook a slow-moving vehicle ahead of me. The road was clear and there were no signs warning of black ice, so I indicated my intentions and accelerated. Having completed my maneuver, I attempted to pull back into my lane. The steering mechanism did not respond in the normal manner, however, and the car began sliding on the icy road toward an embankment that dropped away into a field.

My instinct was to brake sharply and to turn the steering wheel away from the direction I was sliding. But I suddenly remembered something Mr. Westhorpe had taught me ten years earlier regarding what to do if skidding on a wet or icy surface. Somehow I managed to override my instinct, recall the words of instruction, and regain control of the car before it careened off the road. I was so grateful to Mr. Westhorpe and for the principle that permits us to treasure up information in our minds so that important things can be brought to our remembrance.

These illustrations relate to temporal lessons, but there is an even more significant spiritual application. We have been promised that when we have to make decisions, particularly in matters of great consequence, the Holy Ghost will bring all things to our remembrance (see John 14:26). Information gleaned from sacrament meetings, Sunday School classes, and individual and family scripture reading—all enhanced through discussion and pondering—can produce a vast reservoir from which we can draw living water when needed. If we resist the temptation to discount or disregard counsel that does not immediately appear to apply to our circumstances, and instead treasure up the words of life as found in the scriptures and in the writings and talks of living prophets, that portion shall be given us in the very hour that we need it (see D&C 84:85).

Since our thoughts are the sum of everything we put into our minds, we can also pollute that reservoir by introducing inappropriate materials through the things we watch, listen to, read, or think about. We are also influenced in positive or negative ways by those with whom we associate. I discovered many years ago the value of filling the reservoir of my mind with inspirational passages and uplifting statements. I have discovered what is an inextricable link between what we think and the people we become. If we eat impure or unhealthy food, our bodies lose their vitality and cease to function as they should. I believe our minds respond in a similar manner—being strengthened by good thoughts but becoming impaired by exposure to that which is inappropriate or unseemly.

I have found that pursuing a regular routine of physical activity is also beneficial. Exercise invigorates both body and mind and reduces feelings of lethargy. I have found it useful to combine physical exercise with mental development by memorizing passages of scripture or inspired statements while exercising. The process of pondering wholesome thoughts and profound words develops a greater depth of wisdom that regenerates the mind, producing a positive attitude accompanied by a deep sense of security. The Lord has promised: "Treasure up these words in thy heart. Be faithful and diligent in keeping the commandments of God, and I will encircle thee in the arms of my love" (D&C 6:20).

## SUSTAINED BY THE TESTIMONY OF OTHERS

During the formative years of my developing faith and somewhat tentative testimony, I was so grateful for the fulfillment of the promise extended in the scriptures: "For all have not every gift given unto them; for there are many gifts, and to every man is given a gift by the Spirit of God. To some is given one, and to some is given another, that all may be profited thereby. To some it is given by the Holy Ghost to know that Jesus Christ is the Son of God, and that he was crucified for the sins of the world. To others, it is given to believe on their words, that they also might have eternal life if they continue faithful" (D&C 46:11-14).

Initially, I believed the words of others, using scriptures in the context I had heard others use them and quoting the prophets. Over the years, as I treasured up these things, I gained my own witness. The words I speak today may seem comparable to the words I spoke as an early convert, but the depth of my feelings has increased dramatically. My words have become the expression of personal testimony even when I use the scriptures or statements of others. The promise to those who believe "on their words" is "that they also might have eternal life if they continue faithful." We know that eternal life is to "know thee the only true God, and Jesus Christ, whom thou hast sent" (John 17:3).

We progress from the childlike state of total dependence, comparable to a newborn child in the care of parents, to a state of spiritual maturity in which we can stand in the strength of our own knowledge. As we grow from strength to strength, we do well to avoid becoming arrogant. King Benjamin reminds us that we will always be dependent on God: "I say unto you that if ye should serve him who has created you from the beginning, and is preserving you from day to day, by lending you breath, that ye may live and move and do according to your own will, and even supporting you from one moment to another—I say, if ye should serve him with all your whole souls yet ye would be unprofitable servants" (Mosiah 2:21).

## OUR DEPENDENCE ON THE LORD

We depend on the Lord not only for our temporal needs, but for understanding as well: "O the vainness, and the frailties, and the foolishness of men! When they are learned they think they are wise, and they hearken not unto the counsel of God, for they set it aside, supposing they know of themselves, wherefore, their wisdom is foolishness and it profiteth them not. And they shall perish. But to be learned is good if they hearken unto the counsels of God" (2 Nephi 9:28-29).

Gospel study is not to be pursued for academic achievement or to attract acclaim. Paul lamented those who are "ever learning, and never able to come to the knowledge of the truth" (2 Timothy 3:7), and in the Old Testament we are admonished that "wisdom is the principal thing; therefore get wisdom: and with all thy getting get understanding" (Proverbs 4:7). With so many conflicting ideas and diverse opinions abroad in the world, how can we in reality comprehend what is truth? These words of counsel, given to Oliver Cowdery, have been invaluable to me in my pursuit of and desire for understanding: "Behold, you have not understood; you have supposed that I would give it unto you, when you took no thought save it was to ask me. But, behold, I say unto you, that you must study it out in your mind; then you must ask me if it be right, and if it is right I will cause that your bosom shall burn within you; therefore, you shall feel that it is right" (D&C 9:7-8).

## INSTRUCTION AND EDIFICATION

Study is necessary, pondering is required, and treasuring up the truths we discover will increase our intelligence, thereby improving our ability to apply the knowledge we have gained.

Ammon's exuberant expressions reflect the sentiments of all who have experienced the priceless privilege of being "taught from on high" (D&C 43:16). Rejoicing in the gospel and in his love for God, Ammon joyfully proclaimed the source of his understanding: "I do not boast in my own strength, nor in my own wisdom; but behold, my joy is full, yea, my heart is brim with joy, and I will rejoice in my God. Yea, I know that I am nothing; as to my strength I am weak; therefore I will not boast of myself, but I will boast of my God, for in his strength I can do all things" (Alma 26:11-12). Such is the disposition of "the peaceable followers of Christ" (Moroni 7:3).

Having such an outlook, we do not profess greater knowledge than another or aspire for recognition and acclaim but rather yearn for the fulfillment of this promise in our teaching opportunities: "Wherefore, he that preacheth [gives instruction] and he that receiveth, understand one another, and both are edified and rejoice together" (D&C 50:22).

The value of treasuring up in our minds the words of life continually cannot be overestimated. Doing so elevates our minds beyond the realms of normal capacity and puts us in touch with the source of inspiration.

## TREASURE UP AND PONDER

An integral element of treasuring up is pondering. By pondering, we open ourselves to increased understanding; that is, as we reflect on gospel truths, our minds are opened to inspiration. President Joseph F. Smith provides some insight into how this principle operates. He wrote: "On the third of October, in the year nineteen hundred and eighteen, I sat in my room *pondering* over the scriptures; and *reflecting* upon the great atoning sacrifice that was made by the Son of God, for the redemption of the world; And the great and wonderful love made manifest by the Father and the Son in the coming of the Redeemer into the world. That through his atonement, and by obedience to the principles of the gospel, mankind might be saved" (D&C 138:1-4; emphasis added). President Smith then explains that his mind "reverted" to the writings of Peter in the New Testament, which is to say, he began *thinking about* things he had *previously read.* He explains further, "I opened the Bible and read [again] the third and fourth chapters of the first epistle of Peter, and as I read I was greatly impressed, *more than I had ever been before"* (D&C 138:6; emphasis added).

Then he describes what transpired: "As I pondered over these things which are written, the eyes of my understanding were opened, and the Spirit of the Lord rested upon me, and I saw the hosts of the dead, both small and great. And there were gathered together in one place an innumerable company of the spirits of the just, who had been faithful in the testimony of Jesus while they lived in mortality; . . . All these had departed the mortal life, firm in the hope of a glorious resurrection, through the grace of God the Father and his Only Begotten Son, Jesus Christ. I beheld that they were filled with joy and gladness, and were rejoicing together because the day of their deliverance was at hand. They were assembled awaiting the advent of the Son of God into the spirit world, to declare their redemption from the bands of death. Their sleeping dust was to be restored unto its perfect frame, bone to his bone, and the sinews and the flesh upon them, the spirit and the body to be united never again to be divided, that they might receive a fulness of joy" (D&C 138:11-17).

Through the process of pondering and treasuring up the words of life, we too can learn things of the Spirit. "Which things also we speak, not in the words which man's wisdom teacheth, but which the Holy Ghost teacheth; comparing spiritual things with spiritual. But the natural man receiveth not the things of the Spirit of God: for they are foolishness unto him: neither can he know them, because they are spiritually discerned" (1 Corinthians 2:13-14).

The Savior reemphasized these principles in a powerful way when he said: "Hearken ye to these words. Behold, I am Jesus Christ, the Savior of the world. Treasure these things up in your hearts, and let the solemnities of eternity rest upon your minds" (D&C 43:34).

# "I CANNOT SAY
# THE SMALLEST PART
# WHICH I FEEL"

## TEMPORAL APPLICATION OF ETERNAL PRINCIPLES

We strengthen our faith by overcoming difficulties and facing up to challenges. Just as metal is tempered and made strong when heated in a furnace and then quenched in water, so we rise to the heights of our potential as children of God through enduring the experiences that stretch and try us. Perhaps these homely examples from my life will help illustrate what I mean.

In my early teenage years, I enjoyed cycling. It was exhilarating to travel the picturesque country lanes and coastal highways of my native England. I loved the beautiful scenery—the tapestry of trees, fragrant flowers, blue skies, and green fields that provided the backdrop for my journeys. I experienced a particular pleasure and feeling of renewal standing at the seashore at daybreak or sunset, when there were few distractions and I was able to listen to the soothing sound of the sea gently caressing the sand.

Beyond these pleasures, I enjoyed a deep sense of satisfaction and accomplishment as I perfected my cycling skills and increased my endurance by long hours of practice.

In those days I didn't have sufficient money to purchase a cycle such as I would like to have owned. Instead, for very little money, I purchased used cycles or watched for those that had been discarded. Dismantling the parts, I stripped paint off or cleaned the metal components, then built a succession of renovated bikes. This involved cleaning rust from chrome fittings and wheel rims, hand-painting the surfaces, and adjusting or replacing mechanical parts and tires.

Over a number of years, I repeated this process several times, creating an improved version each time. Four decades later, I still get a thrill when I recall what I was able to accomplish with what were literally discarded cycles. There is something very gratifying about the creative process and the feelings associated with creative efforts.

I had much the same feeling of accomplishment as I worked to obtain a testimony of the restored gospel. Step by step and little by little, I acquired the knowledge that served as the basis of my growing faith. In saying this, I realize how difficult it is to convey such feelings to someone who hasn't experienced the joy associated with a growing testimony. A testimony is a deeply personal thing, and only those who have one will understand what I am saying. Though Sir Winston Churchill possibly had something different in mind than a spiritual awakening, he expressed a great truth when he said, "The heart has reasons of which the mind is not aware." We often have feelings and impressions that bring assurance beyond our level of knowledge.

## THE COVENTRY EAGLE BICYCLE

While attending college, I obtained employment delivering newspapers. I was also responsible for maintaining the delivery cycles used by the other young men who were employed by the newsagent. These cycles were fitted with a tubular frame over the front wheel in which a cardboard box could be placed to transport the newspapers.

One Saturday morning as I was delivering newspapers, a Coventry Eagle racing cycle displayed in the window of a cycle shop attracted my attention. With its frame painted a lilac color and with contrasting black accessories, sparkling chrome fittings, and a set of ten-speed derailleur gears, it was a magnificent machine. Admiring its exquisite lines and features, I was filled with an overwhelming desire to own it.

I later told my father about the bike and shared with him my longing to possess it. He asked me how much the cycle cost, but I could scarcely bear to tell him. We were not wealthy, and purchasing such an extravagant machine seemed out of the question. However, Father surprised me by saying he would give the matter some consideration.

The next day he put the following proposal to me: If I would save half the purchase price, he would provide the balance. I had never really thought that there was even the slightest possibility of being able to realize my dreams. My excitement was such that I did not immediately appreciate the full implications of my father's wise proposition. It would take me several months to save up my portion. It wasn't until years later that I realized that my father also needed time to save the amount he had offered to contribute.

Many times while I was saving money, I would pass by the shop, stopping to admire the cycle displayed in the window and hoping it would still be there when I was in a position to make my purchase. The day finally arrived when I had accumulated the required amount, and we were able to buy it. The effort required to earn the money and the amount of time I had waited to acquire the cycle made it all the more precious to me. I took immaculate care of it, keeping it in excellent working order and even drying it down when it got wet in order to preserve its pristine condition.

A testimony, if it is to be treasured, also has to be earned and thereafter nurtured. The happiness I felt in preparing to, and actually being able to, purchase the cycle is minuscule when compared to the joy I experienced in acquiring my testimony of the restored gospel.

## THE HILLMAN MINX CAR

On a Sunday in February 1966, while I was serving as a counselor in a branch presidency, a meeting was scheduled for priesthood leaders at the Hyde Park chapel in London, which was some 120 miles from my home. I owned at the time a black 1957 Hillman Minx car and offered to provide transportation for three other brethren. The journey from Norwich to London was uneventful until we reached Fleet Street, where the offices of the major British national newspapers were located and which was a hub of activity Monday through Friday but largely deserted on a Sunday morning.

After pulling away from a stop light in that area, I found I was unable to engage second gear. We made a brief check of the clutch and gear mechanism, then phoned the Hyde Park chapel for assistance. Brother Arthur Gibbs came to our rescue, picking us up and taking us to the meeting.

We left my treasured Hillman Minx parked at the curbside on Fleet Street. After the meetings had concluded, Brother Gibbs drove us back to my vehicle. We again tried unsuccessfully to engage the gears. Brother Gibbs was a member of the Automobile Association and suggested that we seek the association's assistance even though it was AA policy to provide such service only for members of the organization. I walked with Brother Gibbs to a nearby telephone kiosk and stood by his side as he made the call.

I was only able to hear his end of the conversation and was

surprised when he said, "My friend is a member of the MIA, and his car has a mechanical fault and is parked on Fleet Street. Could you offer him assistance?" After he had replaced the telephone handset, I asked him what the response had been.

He replied, "They are dispatching a mechanic."

I then asked him why he had referred to the MIA and what that had to do with the AA He wasn't aware of what he had said and responded with a look of puzzlement. I then rehearsed with him what I had heard him say in his telephone conversation. He chuckled and said he could only surmise that since he had led a discussion relating to the Mutual Improvement Association in the meeting we had just attended, the subject had been on his mind.

The mechanic arrived and conducted an inspection of the clutch mechanism. He concluded that the clutch pads were worn out and would need to be replaced. He suggested that we leave the car where it was overnight and arrange to have it towed to a garage on Monday morning. Leaving a vehicle on the streets of London overnight seemed to me to be fraught with unpleasant possibilities. While I pondered what to do, two of my traveling companions expressed their condolences and walked away in the direction of the Liverpool Street Railway Station. In an expression of moral support, the other brother stayed with me. After a time, I determined that I would not leave my black Hillman Minx in those circumstances.

When I expressed my reluctance to leave the car on the street, the mechanic said, "There is one other possibility. A vehicle can be driven with an inoperative clutch, but it is very difficult."

I asked if he had ever done so. He said he had, and I asked if he would demonstrate the technique so that I could at least make an attempt to mobilize the vehicle. I sat beside him as he maneuvered along a short stretch of Fleet Street, circling around traffic bollards before returning to where we had originally parked. Seeing the car in motion, the two brethren who had headed for the railway station hurried back to find out what had happened.

## A REMARKABLE RETURN JOURNEY

The four of us settled back in the vehicle, and I pulled away. Shifting gears did generate some grinding sounds, but we were on the way home. I have never checked the number of traffic signals on the route from Fleet Street through the city of London to the A11 Road leading to Norwich, but on that day we did not encounter even one red light.

The next morning I drove my Hillman to the local garage where I had it regularly serviced and maintained. Reaching the forecourt, the Hillman rolled to a stop but would not move an inch more. The clutch mechanism and pads had to be replaced, but we had completed our journey back from London.

## A SPIRITUAL PARALLEL

I have since reflected on the experience and found in it a spiritual parallel. My feelings with regard to leaving the car overnight parked on Fleet Street had been different from those of my traveling companions. Because the car belonged to me, I was not willing to abandon it or risk having it stolen or damaged. The same principle applies to our testimonies. A testimony is not normally easily obtained, a fact that makes its possession all the more precious. That is why once gained and continually nurtured, a personal witness is not easily deserted.

Though very real, a witness of the truth is not *tangible* in the normal sense of the word. In describing his conversion, Amulek reminds us that our testimonies are more a function of the heart than the brain. Having seen much of the power of God, Amulek confesses: "Nevertheless, I did harden my heart, for I was called many times and I would not hear; therefore I knew concerning these things, yet I would not know; therefore I went on rebelling against God" (Alma 10:6). With regard to his testimony, Ammon declared, "Behold, I say unto you, I cannot say the smallest part which I *feel*" (Alma 26:16; emphasis added). All of us who have a testimony often feel more than we can express.

## DISCERNING DETERIORATION

Later that year, I sold the Hillman Minx and upgraded my vehicle to a 1962 Vauxhall Victor Estate. Shortly after making the transaction, the man who had purchased the Hillman phoned to ask me if I had experienced any difficulty steering the vehicle. I told him that I had not but then recalled that I had found the Vauxhall to have far more responsive steering than my Hillman. The new owner agreed to bring the Hillman to my business office so he could demonstrate the difficulty he was having. Once I was seated in the car and had driven it a short distance, I realized how rigid the steering mechanism was. I concluded that during the time I had owned the vehicle, the mechanism had deteriorated so gradually that I had not detected the change. I agreed that the steering was defective and ended up taking responsibility for making the needed repairs.

The experience provided an interesting lesson. I have known some individuals whose testimonies are founded on one inspirational event that they rely upon to sustain them. This is unwise. Just as our bodies require daily nourishment in order to function properly, so do our testimonies need ongoing nourishment. Without regular renewal through prayer, scripture study, partaking of the sacrament, and involvement in Church activity and service, our testimonies are subject to gradual deterioration. Immediate weakening may be so slight as to be imperceptible, but over time we can become bereft of our faith and find ourselves spiritually malnourished.

I find it spiritually stimulating to contemplate the restoration of the gospel and the doctrines that have been revealed in connection with the Lord's "great plan of happiness" (Alma 42:8). Pondering the principles and discussing the doctrines of the kingdom generate within me an excitement that Jeremiah described as "a burning fire shut up in [his] bones" (Jeremiah 20:9). But I have found that such feelings and the teachings that evoke them are not automatically appreciated by others.

## FACTS AND FEELINGS

On many occasions, I have not immediately comprehended what I was being taught. This has also occurred with others when I have tried to share my knowledge. It can be difficult to communicate to someone else what you have learned.

The difficulties associated with transmitting thoughts and sharing knowledge was brought home to me while teaching a course on the principles of color theory to a class of college printing students. I was trying to communicate how the primary colors of red, yellow, and blue, along with white and black, could be blended to match any hue. I explained the theory, demonstrated the process, and then invited each student to match a color sample I had prepared.

The exercise was initially unsuccessful. Not one of the students was able to produce an acceptable match. I repeated the exercise, describing again every aspect of what I was doing to achieve an accurate result. While doing so, I realized there was one thing I had not previously shared with them. If they were to master the technique, the students not only had to know which colors to mix in which proportions, but they had to develop a certain "sense" of what needed to be done. Without that sensitivity to the subtle nuances of shade and tone, they would be unable to master the technique. In simple terms, an understanding of the theory was insufficient; they had to be taught how to acquire this intuitive eye. This process proved to be the most critical and difficult part of teaching the class.

So it is with our understanding of gospel principles. The doctrine may make sense, even be appealing to us, but it cannot be fully understood and believed until we are touched by the Holy Spirit and made to "feel" its truth. That is what Ammon was trying to communicate when he said, "I cannot say the smallest part that I feel" (Alma 26:16).

Adversity also often plays a part in helping to forge our testimonies. Character and testimony are molded by the tests and challenges we meet and overcome. Such tempering makes it possible for us to rise above selfishness and self-interest and reach our full potential.

## TITHING, A TEST OF FAITH

In January 1970, Pamela and I brought our son, Kevin, to Salt Lake City, seeking advice concerning Kevin's health from doctors at the Primary Children's Hospital. To help cover the cost of our journey, we rented our home to a couple and sold some of our personal belongings. My father had also loaned us £50 ($75). Our trip proved fruitful. Kevin's condition was diagnosed, and through a sequence of miraculous events the doctors at the Primary Children's Hospital referred us to a Dr. David Matthews, a Harley Street specialist in London, who agreed to provide ongoing medical care to Kevin on our return to England.

While in Utah for the medical evaluation, we were the recipients of a great many kindnesses, including an apartment provided by Lily May Crotch, whom we had met through her brother Bill Crotch and his wife, Marj, with whom we also stayed for a while. These generous folks had all grown up in our home city of Norwich before immigrating to the United States, and they were friends of Pamela's parents.

One night Pamela and I had an important discussion. Though we were in the country on a temporary visitor's visa, I had obtained permission from government officials in Washington, D.C., to work at Deseret Press during our stay in the United States. Since we depended on that income to meet our expenses, it was a beneficial arrangement. We knew that airfare increased for the summer season at the end of May, and so it was important for us to return to England as soon as possible, both to avoid additional expenses and to commence Kevin's treatments. As Pamela and I reflected on our circumstances, it was clear that if we were to pay tithing on the paycheck I had just received, we would not be able to save enough money to pay our passage home until after ticket prices increased, and we would be delayed in our return journey for several months.

In Pamela's mind there was nothing to debate. We would pay the tithing. Encouraged by her attitude and expression of faith, I agreed. Considering this a private matter, we did not discuss our situation with anyone else.

The next evening we attended a gathering at Lily May's home. She had invited a total of thirty-six people who had previously lived in Norwich. We enjoyed reminiscing with the group, and Pamela and I responded to questions relating to the city they had once called home. At the close of the evening, we were handed a white envelope, which Pamela and I opened after returning to our apartment. We were astonished to find that it contained exactly twice the amount of money we had contributed in tithing, demonstrating once again that "ye receive no witness until after the trial of your faith" (Ether 12:6).

Faith is strengthened by overcoming difficulties and facing

up to challenges. So we rise to the heights of our potential as children of God as a result of our trials. In this chapter I have endeavored to communicate things that are difficult to discern and have come to the conclusion that "I cannot say the smallest part that I feel."

# PERCEPTIONS
# ON PARENTING

## A PROMISE TO PARENTS

In an earlier chapter I described the manner in which an Apostle once taught me a great principle. Using his thumb and forefinger, he indicated that only a small amount of information I would need as a General Authority would come from here on earth. The greater portion, he said, would come from heaven, testifying thereby that the most important source of learning is inspiration. Through personal experiences, I have gained a certain knowledge of this principle and of the reality that blessings of inspiration are not exclusively reserved for Church leaders.

Some of my most significant inspirational experiences have occurred in fulfilling my sacred responsibilities as a husband and father. It has become obvious to me that a loving Father in Heaven would not entrust his spirit children to the care of mortal parents without providing a means by which mothers and fathers could receive guidance and inspiration from a divine source. Just as we seek inspiration in preparing to teach a lesson or present a message in a church meeting, we ought to ask for divine help in planning family home evenings and in making decisions of importance to family members.

## LEARNING AS A FAMILY

Pamela has a wonderful talent for communicating with young children, which has enabled us to enjoy many memorable family home evenings. On one occasion she cut three silhouette figures, representing a mother, father, and a child, out of the *Family Home Evening Resource Book*. Our son, Kevin, had not yet mastered the art of speaking, but Pamela wanted to teach him that families need to be whole and can be eternal.

She first linked just the figures representing the mother and the child, then waited for Kevin's reaction. Turning his head from side to side, he indicated that something was amiss. The cut-out figures were then rearranged to represent the father and the child linked together. This brought the same negative response from Kevin as before, as he indicated his dissatisfaction. Finally, Pamela linked all three figures together, and Kevin nodded his approval with a smile of satisfaction. Even at such a young age he was able to comprehend the notion of a united family.

I am convinced it is necessary to teach fundamental truths to children according to their ability to comprehend and not to avoid questions or give false information. Using this approach, we can then build from a sure foundation.

## TEACHING BY EXAMPLE

Children observe what their parents do and are inclined to impersonate what they see. The importance of example in teaching children should not be overlooked. For example, when walking hand-in-hand on shopping expeditions with Kevin, I would cross the road only at light-controlled or marked crossings. It troubled me that many parents would, if the road was clear, lead their children across the road, disregarding a red light. I wanted to teach Kevin more than simply how to safely negotiate a crossing. I wanted to prepare him for occasions when he would, in later years, be unaccompanied. I was also interested in providing him a sense of self-discipline, including the desire to honor laws and observe ethical values.

Because it is important to respect the possessions of others, Pamela and I resolved never to use a pen, a sheet of paper, or anything belonging to Kevin without first obtaining his permission—even when he was very young. We believe this approach helped him develop a respect for and appreciation of property and objects belonging to others. Now an adult himself, Kevin never even uses the telephones in our home when visiting without first asking permission to do so. Having such respect for others is the core of good character.

Children can be very effective teachers. Once while Kevin was spending the night with his grandparents, my mother knelt with him to listen to his prayers. He surprised her by saying, "It's your turn to pray." When Mother confessed, "I don't know how to pray." Kevin patiently explained, "You say, Heavenly Father, thank him for the blessings you have received, ask him for the things you need, and say in the name of Jesus Christ." Mother told me that this was the first time in her life she had really prayed, and from that point forward, she continued to pray in that manner before she retired each night.

Another example of the influence a child can have occurred in our family when young Kevin told his grandfather, "It's not good to smoke cigarettes," and appealed to him not to do so. My father was so affected by the request that he stopped smoking, a remarkable thing since he had previously failed many times in such attempts. The sincerity of a child's plea can be more effective than the eloquence of adult reasoning.

## ASSUMPTIONS AND MISUNDERSTANDINGS

One of the qualities that I consider essential to achieving a happy marriage and becoming a successful parent is the ability to communicate. It is unwise to just assume that our spouse or our children understand what we have said or fully grasp the reality of a circumstance.

This became evident to me in 1970 when I was called to serve as a counselor in a district presidency. Three districts had been combined in anticipation of the creation of a new stake, and the resulting district encompassed a large geographical area. Attending to the needs of the district was taking up a great deal of my time, and in the six weeks following the creation of the new district, I had been gone from home for most of each Sunday.

As I returned from one of those long Sabbath excursions, Pamela suggested that it would be wise to make my new calling the subject of our family home evening discussion the next night. Her attention had been drawn to the need to do so by a question posed by Kevin: "Why does Daddy go to work on Sundays now?" To his three-year-old mind, I was doing what I did during the week–leaving home for the office in the morning and returning home in the evening. Yes, he had been in the meeting when I had been sustained, and we had already discussed Daddy's new assignment, but clearly we had not communicated the implications. His question provided an excellent teaching opportunity, but I learned a greater lesson. If I had taken more time to view the situation from his perspective, a misunderstanding would not have occurred.

As a result of this experience, the counsel given to parents in Deuteronomy 6:7 became much more significant to me: "And thou shalt teach [my words] *diligently* unto thy children, and shalt talk of them when thou sittest in thine house, and when thou walkest by the way, and when thou liest down, and when thou risest up" (emphasis added).

Seven years later, I had another experience that caused me to consider more deeply the importance of effective communication. Pamela was involved in a leadership meeting at the chapel, which meant Kevin and I had an evening to spend together. I asked him what he would like to do. Knowing that I was considering a change of motor vehicle, he suggested we might visit some automobile showrooms.

During the years when we were working to establish a business, we had always purchased previously owned, modestly priced cars that were several years old. However, our accountant had recently informed me that the time had come to upgrade the image of the company. He recommended I buy a more modern motor vehicle and indicated there were funds enough to do so. He had even calculated an amount I might spend on a new car.

I had not explained any of this to Kevin and so when I approached a vehicle in the car showroom that was only three years old and carried a purchase price more than double what I had previously paid, Kevin immediately cautioned me, "Dad, you can't afford to look at that car!" My response was a smile as I began to examine the vehicle. In agitated tones, Kevin tried to attract my attention to an older, less expensive model. By then I had opened the car door and was inspecting the interior, but Kevin was standing well away from the vehicle, as if approaching it were as an inappropriate thing to do.

His next communication was an audible whisper, the kind you would normally associate with someone keeping watch while a colleague commits a felony.

"Dad! The salesman is coming!"

Not wishing to prolong Kevin's anxiety, I walked over to where he was standing and reassured him that we were in a position to consider purchasing a vehicle such as the one I was inspecting. His concerns were immediately allayed, and he joined me in excitedly examining the external and interior features of the car. I had not anticipated his initial reaction to my interest in the vehicle but was delighted with the evidence of his maturity and his impulse to protect me from the consequences of what to him, with limited information, would have been an unwise decision.

## THE PAINTING PROJECT

Spending time together and participating in projects provides opportunities for learning experiences that build father-and-son relationships. When Kevin was a young boy, the exterior woodwork of our home was in need of repainting. I cleaned and prepared the surface and applied an undercoat. In my mind I could visualize the flawless glossy finish that would be the product of my labors. Kevin watched as I prepared to apply the final gloss covering. When he asked if he could help me, I hesitated, considering what effect this would have on the fulfillment of my goal and how he would feel if I declined his offer.

It was almost as if I heard someone else say, "That would be a great help. Thank you."

After I provided him with an old shirt of mine that covered him completely, almost touching the floor, and with the sleeves folded back several times, we went to work on the front door of our home. While I worked on the top section of the door, Kevin was earnestly applying paint to the bottom. He was doing well for his age and size, but his effort was understandably less than professional, and some of the paint on his part of the door was running. Wanting to ensure the door was uniformly painted, each time he bent to recharge his brush, I would hastily smooth out the paint on the bottom panel, then return to my own area, hoping he would not realize what I was doing.

I decided that the opportunity of working with my son was more important than assuring a first-class paint job. Besides, he was doing amazingly well, and I gave up on smoothing his work. Thereafter, every time I approached the door and saw the distinctive style of decorating, I was reminded of what is really important in our lives. I was satisfied that the association is far more important than the project. The strength of the bond endures long after the paint has flaked and separated from the surface it once protected.

The learning experiences Kevin and I shared were of a temporal nature but with spiritual connotations. Over the years we also participated together in performing sacred ordinances and making covenants through which the power of godliness was manifest.

## TEACHING OUR CHILDREN THE GOSPEL

As previously indicated, Pamela was reared and nurtured in an LDS family where the principles of the restored gospel were taught. When I first encountered the Church, she helped me appreciate the value of such things as family prayer, family home evening, and family councils. We determined early in our marriage that it was our responsibility to teach the gospel to our son, and from Kevin's earliest years we taught him the doctrines relating to baptism, the gift of the Holy Ghost, priesthood ordinations, patriarchal blessings, and temple and mission preparation. We taught these things in our home and depended on the meetings and classes at Church only to complement that which we were learning together as a family.

When he was a boy, Kevin often accompanied his mother in her Relief Society work as she visited the sick and the elderly to administer compassionate service. He and I would also later be home teaching companions, which provided many wonderful opportunities for us to share spiritual experiences. In these settings, he was learning gospel principles through practical application.

## LEARNING TO CHOOSE THE RIGHT

Children can learn important lessons when given the opportunity to make decisions in what might appear to be relatively unimportant matters. As parents, our aim was to have our son one day officiate in the ordinances of the Aaronic Priesthood in preparation for receiving the Melchizedek Priesthood and entering the temple and serving a mission. We thought it wise to instill in him an understanding of future expectations to avoid the need to make last-minute adjustments. One of our practices was to provide Kevin a white shirt for Sunday attire from the time he was an infant. As he matured to the point where he was old enough to make decisions, Pamela would lay out on his bed a selection of clothing from which he could choose what to wear. On Sunday there would be a white shirt and dark blue, gray, or black trousers with a necktie to match the color of the trousers chosen. Offering him a choice from three acceptable options permitted him some independence while he practiced making his own decisions—something he would need to know how to do in later life.

One such situation occurred when Kevin was a teenager and a member of the school basketball team that won the right to compete in a league championship game. Unfortunately, the game was scheduled to be played on a Sunday. That represented a conflict with our principles and required our family to make a decision. After discussing the matter fully, Kevin ended up voluntarily withdrawing from the team. Although he was disappointed at having to do so, he felt good about making what we all knew to be the right decision—a decision he might not have made had it not been for prior preparation.

The practice of teaching Kevin correct principles in his early years helped significantly through his teenage years. At age eighteen Kevin would still ask what time I wanted him to return home when he was going out with friends. I would respond, "What time do you think you should come home?" His response would often be in the form of a question. "Would eleven o'clock be okay?" That would allow me to ratify his decision or to discuss options, should that be necessary.

Whenever there was a significant decision to be made, we would ponder and pray together—when considering the purchase of a motor vehicle or what music was appropriate to listen to and many other things. Those shared experiences have contributed to a close family relationship that has flourished through the years.

## LOVE UNFEIGNED

Sharing successes and overcoming obstacles together binds family members. In the hymn "Know This, That Every Soul Is Free" (Hymns, no. 240), we find the words, "He'll call, persuade, direct aright, And bless with wisdom, love, and light, In nameless ways be good and kind, But never force the human mind." This manner of influence is tenderly expressed in D&C 121:41: "No power or influence can or ought to be maintained by virtue of the priesthood, only by persuasion, by long-suffering, by gentleness and meekness, and by love unfeigned." Unfeigned means genuine or sincere. When we sincerely love someone, our love tempers the way we treat them. I am not advocating the abdication of parental responsibility in directing and disciplining children, but I do believe that such correction should be motivated by love and characterized by kindness. The scriptures disclose the feelings of the Lord in such matters: "For whom the Lord loveth he chasteneth." The passage goes on to say, "Furthermore we have had fathers of our flesh which corrected us, and we gave them reverence: shall we not much rather be in subjection [submissive] unto the Father of spirits, and live?" (Hebrews 12:6, 9). The words "and live" suggest the idea that such chastisement is for our benefit and well-being.

In the difficult moments that occur in raising children, we should never lose sight of the long-term objectives. No matter how agitated we may become, we must not act unwisely or harshly in our desire to make a point, curtail foolish behavior, or resolve a situation. I am grateful to have learned this principle through my Church service experiences and to have been able to apply it in my duties as a father.

## DESIRES AND DECISIONS

One of our fondest hopes as parents was that our son would one day serve a mission. Over the years, we took every opportunity to plant and nurture that seed in Kevin. One of the things that proved useful in this regard was the father's interviews I conducted with him prior to such significant events as baptism, priesthood ordinations, etc. As far as I could determine, Kevin was on track to accept a mission call when he reached the appropriate age.

As he approached his nineteenth birthday, I was serving as stake president. Prior to then, we had devoted many family home evening discussions to the subject of missionary service. The week before Kevin was scheduled to meet with the bishop to finalize his missionary recommendation forms, we sat together, and I conducted yet another father's interview. It was a joyous occasion, concluding with hugs and expressions of love and appreciation.

Following his interview with Kevin, our bishop was thoughtful enough to phone me to share his observations on how well prepared our son was for missionary service. We then made arrangements for my interview with him as the stake president. Given the preparations we had made and Kevin's seeming willingness to serve, I anticipated that this meeting would in many ways be a formality.

Kevin and I met in the stake president's office and reviewed his worthiness. All went well until Kevin posed a penetrating question, "Do I have to serve a mission?" This was totally unexpected. I had not even considered the possibility, but I said that he could not be compelled to serve. I did remind him that the Lord, through his prophets, had revealed that every worthy, healthy, and mentally capable young man is expected to serve.

Kevin then asked, "What would people think if the stake president's son did not serve as a missionary?" It was obvious that even after years of preparation, Kevin was not yet ready to embark on the Lord's errand with full purpose of heart. I expressed my hope that he not serve because of the expectations of others but because he wanted to. Since he was clearly not ready to make a commitment, I suggested that we review the situation in thirty days. He agreed, and we concluded the formal interview.

Though Pamela and I discussed the situation with some concern, life in our home followed a familiar pattern and was not unduly disrupted by what had happened. As parents we prayed for support and guidance in how to appropriately influence Kevin to make the right decision. However, when we met for our second formal interview, Kevin once again displayed his reluctance to send in his missionary papers.

He inquired what would happen to his motor car. We had sufficient funds in his mission account to support him, so it would not be necessary to sell the vehicle to raise money. But I did not think it wise to keep it for two years and proposed that we offer it for sale, invest the proceeds, and that on his return he purchase a replacement. I had overlooked the car's unique paint work. Kevin reminded me that there were only four cars like it in the entire country. My somewhat frivolous response that maybe he would be able to replace it with a model of which there were only three in the country was not well received.

He then turned his attention to his reluctance to be separated from his friends and pointed out that two years is a long time. I countered by suggesting that he would develop even deeper friendships in the mission field through shared spiritual experiences. None of this helped. It was obvious that Kevin was still struggling with the decision to serve. Without reaching an agreement, we determined to meet again the next month.

The day of our next meeting was a Fast Sunday. Pamela and I were certainly fasting with a purpose, and I had prepared myself to be persuasive and patient, and to demonstrate gentleness, meekness, and love unfeigned in an attempt to influence Kevin to make what I saw as the right decision. We had, of course, discussed the matter again at home, but Kevin had not expressed his feelings. Imagine my surprise and delight when Kevin walked into the stake president's office and with enthusiasm declared, "I'm ready. When can I go?" He had momentarily overlooked the fact that my role was to submit the recommendation, but that the call would come from the Lord through his prophets. We submitted the papers in the normal way, and Kevin soon received his call to serve in the England Leeds Mission.

Many times over the ensuing years, Kevin has remarked, "What if I had passed up the opportunity to serve a mission? It stands as the defining season of my life. All that I had been taught growing up was clarified and confirmed. In the mission field I recognized the potential Heavenly Father had given me, and I gained insights into how to accomplish what is most important in life."

## THE ANSWERS WILL COME
## THROUGH INSPIRATION

My intent in sharing the details of such a personal family experience is not to propose a process or a practice but to reaffirm that the Lord will bless us, both as parents and in our Church assignments, if we will "put [our] trust in that Spirit which leadeth to do good—yea, to do justly, to walk humbly, to judge righteously; and this is my Spirit" (D&C 11:12). Such is the promise of the Lord.

I am impressed with the influence that Helaman had in his parental role. We are told that he had two sons and that "he gave unto the eldest the name of Nephi, and unto the youngest, the name of Lehi. *And they began to grow up unto the Lord*" (Helaman 3:21; emphasis added). I can visualize those sons sitting at the feet of their parents, being taught eternal principles. That they were so taught is later confirmed: "And now, my sons, remember, remember that it is upon the rock of our Redeemer, who is Christ, the Son of God, that ye must build your foundation; that when the devil shall send forth his mighty winds, yea, his shafts in the whirlwind, yea, when all his hail and his mighty storm shall beat upon you, it shall have no power over you to drag you down to the gulf of misery and endless wo, because of the rock upon which ye are built, which is a sure foundation, a foundation whereon if men build they cannot fall." The scriptures further affirm, "These were the words which Helaman taught to his sons; yea, he did teach them many things which are not written" (Helaman 5:12-13).

This illustrates the power that personal testimony can have in our attempts to teach our children the gospel. There is inestimable benefit in sharing our witness of sacred things individually with each child. Though some children may not respond, we see what can happen in the case of Helaman's sons: "And they did *remember* his words; and therefore they went forth, keeping the commandments of God" (Helaman 5:14; emphasis added).

I believe this is the greatest desire of every parent who understands the plan of salvation—that their children might also partake of the gospel and fully embrace the teachings of the Church. The experiences we have enjoyed as a family have given me an insight into the potential that exists for happiness in eternity. The Lord has confirmed the hope that I have for me and my loved ones: "And that same sociality which exists among us here will exist among us there, only it will be coupled with eternal glory, which glory we do not now enjoy" (D&C 130:2).

# THINGS AS THEY REALLY ARE

## THE VIEW BACKSTAGE

In 1964, Kenneth Warren and I launched an insurance business. Initially, our income was modest, and I sought opportunities to supplement it. I was acquainted with Brother Raymond Barber, who was a film projectionist and the manager of lighting for musical and dramatic productions staged at the Theatre Royal in Norwich. When a production came to the theater, additional stagehands were needed, and Brother Barber was influential in helping me get a job moving scenery and props and fulfilling other backstage duties.

The lasting memory I have of this experience is the contrast between the way many of the artists behaved backstage and the transformation they underwent when the curtain rose. Irritable, impolite, and unseemly behavior and hardened faces displayed in the wings were transformed on stage into congeniality, radiant smiles, and endearing manners. Observing this duplicity made me wonder about the sincerity of the great majority of the performers I encountered. Even costumes that looked drab and worn in the wings took on a new luster under the glare of the stage lights. The theater was not a comfortable environment, and I quickly determined not to seek further opportunities to work there; however, I have never forgotten the lessons I learned.

The New Testament warns against inconsistencies between what we are and what we appear to be: "A double-minded man is unstable in all his ways," (James 1:8). And in the Book of Mormon we read: "But behold, I, Jacob, would speak unto you that are pure in heart. Look unto God with firmness of mind, and pray unto him with exceeding faith, and he will console you in your afflictions, and he will plead your cause, . . . O all ye that are pure in heart, lift up your heads and receive the pleasing word of God, and feast upon his love; for ye may, if your minds are firm, forever" (Jacob 3:1-2).

## KISSING MOTHER

To further illustrate that things are not always as they seem in life, consider this experience from my youth.

I was ten or eleven years old, and my brother, Clive, who was three years older than I, offered to take me to the cinema. We had a delightful tradition in our family that whenever we parted from Mother, we would kiss her on the cheek. Before leaving for the picture show, Clive and I came into the kitchen where Mother was doing some ironing. Clive stepped to where she was standing and gently kissed her on the cheek. Then I stepped forward to do the same. As I did so, I felt an intense tingling sensation in my lips—so intense that I jumped away from her. She was also startled and said she had experienced a pricking sensation on her face.

"What happened?" Clive asked.

I said, "When I kissed Mother, I felt an unpleasant sensation in my lips."

My brother insisted it was my imagination and that nothing unusual had happened. To confirm his assessment, he leaned forward and again kissed my mother's cheek. Nothing untoward happened.

Concluding that all was well, I stepped forward and kissed Mother once more. This time the resulting sensation threw me backward. The second incident prompted a serious investigation into the cause. Clive finally surmised that on the two occasions when I had kissed Mother, she was holding the iron; when my brother did so, she was not. Upon checking the iron, it was found to have a fault in the wiring. My contact with her had completed the circuit, causing the electrifying sensation.

At times, if we draw faulty conclusions, we can exclude ourselves from opportunities that would be beneficial. Our misconceptions can be the result of simple ignorance or the product of deceptions practiced by unscrupulous people. To the latter, Isaiah issued this warning: "Woe unto them that call evil good, and good evil; that put darkness for light, and light for darkness; that put bitter for sweet, and sweet for bitter! . . . Which justify the wicked for reward, and take away the righteousness of the righteous from him!" (Isaiah 5:20, 23).

We do well to carefully evaluate the things we encounter in life. An unpleasant experience does not necessarily mean that the activity or organization is bad, and a good experience does not automatically confirm that it is worthy of our continuing participation. For instance, attendance at a Church meeting may not immediately be the most comfortable experience: it takes time to adjust to unfamiliar surroundings, associations with new people, and procedures that are new to us. But in the end, attendance at church may well be one of the most important things we can do. Likewise, the scriptural exhortation to "prove all things; hold fast that which is good" (1 Thessalonians 5:21) does not require us to experiment with things that are obviously inappropriate. Rather, it is an injunction to do what Alma says we ought to do: "Awake and arouse your faculties, even to an experiment upon my words" (Alma 32:27). By so doing, we come to know good from evil, truth from error.

## THE BITTER FRUIT

I recall another experience I had when I was twelve or thirteen. A friend of mine had an uncle who farmed land in an area known as Carey's Meadow. During the summer school break, my friend and I enjoyed playing in the uncle's fields. A favorite spot was a pond that encircled a small island on which grew some trees and other foliage. On one occasion we noticed that one of the trees located on the island was ladened with small apples. They were a magnetic attraction for us.

We discovered that by climbing out on a limb of another tree and leaning precariously over the stagnant water of the pond, we could reach some of the fruit on the tree. After stripping some of the small apples from one of the branches, we sat on the grass to enjoy our bounty. These were wild crab apples, and though they were red, they were so tart as to be inedible. They had looked so inviting; we had embarked on a heroic quest to possess them. Yet they were not at all what they appeared to be. It was just another example of how a misperception can lead to a disappointing discovery.

## PARTAKING OF THE FRUIT OF THE TREE OF LIFE

Some who reach out for the fruits of the gospel find that, for some reason, it is bitter instead of sweet to the taste. The reason is not because the fruit is not ripe, but rather because the individual is not spiritually prepared to partake. In the Book of Mormon, Lehi describes the vision he had of the tree of life. It was a tree "whose fruit was desirable to make one happy," and he discovered that it was "most sweet, above all that [he] ever before tasted." Moreover, partaking of the fruit "filled [his] soul with exceedingly great joy." Lehi's impulse was to share his discovery: "Wherefore, I began to be desirous that my family should partake of it also; for I know that it was desirable above all other fruit" (see 1 Nephi 8:10-12).

I can imagine his disappointment when some of his family did not respond to his invitation to partake of the fruit. He must have been equally surprised to discover that some who partook didn't enjoy the same experience he had: "And after they had tasted of the fruit they were ashamed, because of those that were scoffing at them; and they fell away into forbidden paths and were lost" (1 Nephi 8:28).

Nephi *did* experience the joy described in his father's account. The reason Nephi was susceptible may be found in his own description of that experience: "And it came to pass after I, Nephi, having heard all the words of my father, concerning the things which he saw in a vision, and also the things which he spake by the power of the Holy Ghost, which power he received by faith on the Son of God—and the Son of God was the Messiah who should come—I, Nephi, was desirous also that I might see, and hear, and know of these things, by the power of the Holy Ghost, which is the gift of God unto all those who diligently seek him, as well in times of old as in the time that he should manifest himself unto the children of men. For he is the same yesterday, to-day, and forever; and the way is prepared for all men from the foundation of the world, if it so be that they repent and come unto him" (1 Nephi 10:17-18). Nephi was clearly inclined to believe and sufficiently spiritually attuned to accept the revelation.

The way that truth can be discerned and reality confirmed has been prepared from the foundation of the world. It is by the Spirit of Truth, the Holy Ghost, who the Savior promised "will guide [us] into all truth" (John 16:13).

## FALSE IMPRESSION

We who have taken upon us the name of Christ and presume to be his disciples need to know that our behavior can have a profound impact on those who observe us. In this regard, the scriptures counsel us to "abstain from all appearance of evil" (1 Thessalonians 5:22). I had an experience that illustrates how seemingly innocent actions can create misunderstandings.

I had arranged to pick up Pamela after she had purchased some groceries. We had agreed where to meet, and I had arrived a little earlier than we had planned. I parked next to the curb in front of the store and waited for Pamela to emerge. The sound of the rear nearside door of my vehicle being opened attracted my attention, and I was startled to see a woman I didn't know loading her bags of groceries into the rear seat of my car. Then she proceed to give me instructions as to where she wished me to transport her. My car was black, and I had inadvertently parked in an area reserved for taxis. The lady had drawn an obvious conclusion. She was distraught with me, and I was embarrassed as I apologized to her.

This experience showed how our outward appearance, the places we frequent, and those with whom we associate can contribute to creating false impressions.

Experience has also taught me not to judge situations hastily or without sufficient information. Whenever I am called upon to exercise judgment, I must do so with "kindness, and pure knowledge, which shall greatly enlarge the soul without hypocrisy, and without guile" (D&C 121:42).

## THE OUTWARD APPEARANCE

We can also content ourselves with inferior standards that initially appear to be acceptable until exposed to the test of time. I will use an example from my own life to illustrate what I mean.

At one home where Pamela, Kevin, and I lived, a large, white, six-foot wooden fence surrounded the garden (yard). After a time, the paint began to deteriorate, losing its luster and peeling off in places. A green powdery fungi also appeared on some areas. I decided that the fence needed attention.

Working on just three sections of the fence, I first scraped and sanded the old paint, exposing the bare wood. Then I applied a wood primer, an undercoat of paint, and finally a top coat. The finished result was impressive but had taken me considerable time, and I still had twelve more sections to do. I decided the task would take more time than I could dedicate to the project, unless I could find a way to finish it more quickly. Rather than scrape all the paint off, I determined I would simply brush away the particles of grime and smooth the surface with sandpaper before applying a single coat of paint. Initially, the finished result looked comparable to the first three sections, and I was satisfied with my efforts.

But six weeks later, my paint job began to flake, and the fungi reappeared on the areas of the fence where I had taken the shortcut. The first three sections that I had properly prepared, however, retained a satiny, finished look.

Contemplating the wasted effort and the sorry state of my fence, I thought of what the Lord had once said to Samuel the prophet: "For man looketh on the outward appearance, but the Lord looketh on the heart" (1 Samuel 16:7).

## THINGS OF LASTING WORTH

As with so many things in life, time spent in preparation produces longer-lasting results and in the long run ends up requiring less time.

This experience raised the question of how to discern between what is of lasting worth and what is temporary, insignificant, or even erroneous. If the gospel teaches us anything, it is that truth is not determined by personal preference or popularity. This is easily recognized when we realize that the greatest achievements of mankind result not from *changing* laws but by learning to *comply* with them. The Lord has given us this definition of truth: "And truth is knowledge of things as they are, and as they were, and as they are to come" (D&C 93:24).

We live in perilous times when the truths that provide the pillars of our society are being replaced by fallacies and ungodly philosophies. Family, traditional marriage, fidelity, integrity, chastity, and charity—the values upon which communities and nations must be built—are being discounted and discarded by many as restrictive to their freedom, when in reality they provide the framework for true freedom. After all the intervening years, the words of King Benjamin still ring true: "And moreover, I would desire that ye should consider on the blessed and happy state of those that keep the commandments of God. For behold, they are blessed in all things, both temporal and spiritual; and if they hold out faithful to the end they are received into heaven, that thereby they may dwell with God in a state of never-ending happiness. O remember, remember that these things are true; for the Lord hath spoken it" (Mosiah 2:41).

## COMPARISON WITH CONSTANTS

I reached the pinnacle of my printing career when I became a process prover. As such, it was my responsibility to produce accurate color prints of such things as flower catalogs, picturesque scenes, stately homes, etc. This involved creating a plate in each of four basic colors—chrome yellow, magenta, cyan blue, and black. If one of the colors was too intense, the finished result was unacceptable. To achieve the required results, I used an electronic device known as a densitometer, which projected a beam of light onto a solid printed bar of the color positioned parallel to the image. The meter reading was displayed on a screen and could then be visually compared with predetermined standards for each color. I could recheck the density periodically to ensure that the appropriate standard was being maintained. The proofs that I thus produced would later be used by the printing press operator as his guide.

I had developed a visual sensitivity to the required density of each color, but I still consulted the densitometer. I use this example from my experience in printing because it has a parallel in the way we discern spiritual truth. Just as I could confirm my visual impressions of colors by consulting a densitometer, so can we confirm spiritual truth by an appeal to "the light of truth" (see D&C 124:9). In my quest for understanding, I have found it useful to compare my thoughts and impressions to the scriptures or the words of the prophets. By following this procedure, I replace confusion with conviction and eradicate error with eternal principles of truth.

In the Book of Mormon, the prophet Jacob provides this insight: "Behold, my brethren, he that prophesieth, let him prophesy to the understanding of men; for the Spirit speaketh the truth and lieth not. Wherefore, it speaketh of *things as they really are*, and of things as they really will be; wherefore, these things are manifested unto us plainly, for the salvation of our souls. But behold, we are not witnesses alone in these things; for God also spake them unto prophets of old" (Jacob 4:13; emphasis added).

The search for truth is the innermost quest of the human soul. When we accompany our acquisition of knowledge with righteous application, we recognize *things as they really are*, and peace of conscience is assured.

# THE CAUSE AND
# THE COVENANTS

## ANXIOUSLY ENGAGED

As a young man I enjoyed participating in competitive sporting activities. Though I was three years younger than my brother, Clive, I would often be invited to play football (soccer) with him and his friends. The age difference demanded my best efforts and total exertion to be able to compete.

On one occasion, Clive and I set off to play soccer at the Salhouse Road soccer pitch, which was located four miles from our home. Clive made the journey on a bicycle, and I ran behind him dressed in my football attire, including boots with studs on the soles. After reaching the soccer ground we played for ninety minutes and then returned home in the same manner. I was totally exhausted, to the extent that when I arrived home I collapsed and had to be carried to my bed, where I slept for about twelve hours. Whatever the quality of my performance, I could never be faulted for lack of effort.

The college I attended organized students into four groups or "houses," each of which was designated by a name and traditional color: Blyth (blue), Gannon (green), Ramage (red), and White (white). Each unit had a house captain—a student in his senior year who was appointed to be the leader of, and example for, all the students assigned to that house. A great deal of pride was associated with belonging to one's group, and whenever a student participated in a sporting activity, he would wear the color that identified the house he was representing. I was assigned to the Ramage House.

## CAPTAIN OF RAMAGE HOUSE

The housemaster of Ramage House was Mr. Ben Burgess. Standing six-foot-four, he was a formidable individual. Shortly after the commencement of my final year at the college, I was summoned to Mr. Burgess's office. With great trepidation, I walked the corridors to keep my appointment, and my first knock on his office door was intentionally feeble in the hope that he would not hear and I could return to the classroom without having to face whatever fate awaited me. As I stood waiting, I concluded that this strategy would not succeed, and I knocked a second time more loudly than before.

Mr. Burgess's loud, deep voice invited me to enter. Nervously pushing the door open, I ventured into the room to be greeted with the words, "Ah, Johnson!"

Mr. Burgess then launched into a passionate address in which he expressed his deep feelings about the honor it was to belong to Ramage House. It was all rather overwhelming to the mind of a young student. He continued his discourse, declaring that this would be a year of glory and achievement and that he had chosen me to be house captain. He informed me it would be my duty to lead and motivate the other students to the greatest achievements ever in the storied history of Ramage House.

I am sure Sir Winston Churchill never delivered a more stirring speech. As I recall, I had no opportunity to respond or even express my acceptance. Mr. Burgess simply assumed that I would lead by example and participate in every activity, beginning with the boxing tournament scheduled in four weeks' time.

My senses were dulled as I left his office that day. Was this an honor, or had I simply been chosen to be a sacrifice? The imagery evoked by Sir Winston Churchill in his epic speech did not elude me: "We shall fight them on the beaches." There was no escape. I had two options: One was to disobey Mr. Burgess, which was inconceivable, or to participate in the boxing tournament. The latter was, I concluded, the safer of the two options.

Shortly thereafter, Mr. Burgess organized an assembly of all the students of Ramage House, where he repeated his stirring address, announced my appointment as house captain and my pending participation in the boxing tournament, and invited others to indicate their willingness to participate. There was not an enthusiastic response.

My attitude was not yet comparable with that of David, who, when he saw that the Israelites lacked the courage to face Goliath, uttered the words, "Is there not a cause?" (1 Samuel 17:29). But even though I was a reluctant enrollee, I was already gaining a feeling for the cause and developing a spark of dedication to duty. Eventually, through encouragement, cajoling, and coercion, we assembled sufficient competitors for the boxing tournament.

## THE BOXING TOURNAMENT

Several days after the meeting announcing my appointment, I saw a growing group of students gathered around the college notice board. I walked over to see what had attracted their interest. Standing at the rear of the group and raising myself to the tip of my toes, I scanned the notices and saw one that read, "College Boxing Tournament Bouts." Looking down the list of names, I found my own and was dismayed to see that my opponent was a student named Mike Dewing. I knew him to be an amateur boxer with the Norwich Lads Club.

The day of the boxing tournament arrived, and I traveled to the college with great anxiety. My memories of the actual fight are limited. I know the bout consisted of three rounds of three minutes each, but all I remember of it was being hit in the face once and my hitting something three times. You can imagine my total surprise when at the end of the fight the referee raised my right arm in the air, indicating that I had won.

After returning to the changing room, Mike explained, "I have always had difficulty in dealing with a southpaw."

I responded, "What is a southpaw?"

With a puzzled look on his face he replied, "A boxer who leads with his right hand." Up until that moment, he had believed that I had had some previous boxing experience. Mr. Burgess was elated, and Ramage House had an auspicious beginning for the new year.

## LESSONS IN LEADERSHIP

The college also followed a practice of appointing prefects—twelve students in their senior year who were responsible for helping to maintain discipline and order. As one of the prefects, I was required to wear a distinctive blazer. The regular blazer worn by all students was green; prefects wore a special green blazer that was decorated with a distinctive gold braid edging. My parents could not afford to purchase a new blazer for me, so my father sewed gold braiding on the blazer that I had worn since entering the college. I wore it with honor.

From time to time, the teachers would hold a staff meeting, leaving the prefects to supervise the students for a period of time. On one of those occasions, a winter's day when snow had fallen, the senior prefect determined that the students should spend this time out-of-doors, in the recreation area surrounding the college. He ordered that the doors be closed and that prefects be stationed at the doors to enforce his no-entry ruling.

The door at which I and a fellow prefect were stationed was shaken from the outside by some first-year students who were trying to gain access to the building. I opened the door and explained that students were not allowed back into the building until the staff meeting had concluded. The boys were agitated and complained that they were being harassed by "day-release students" (young men who had concluded their college studies but who were now employed and required to attend day-release classes to gain specialized educational qualifications).

Observing their degree of concern, I inquired of the senior prefect if we might allow these students back into the building. He had no compassion for their plight and declined my request. Motivated by a sense of responsibility, I decided to leave the security of the building so that I could check the circumstances for myself. I invited other prefects to accompany me but received no support. Leaving the building, I accompanied the young men to the area where they claimed senior students had pelted them with snowballs.

My appearing on the scene created a diversion: I was a far more interesting target than the first-year students. The assailants converged upon me and rolled me in the snow like a human snowball and then made a hasty retreat. I had achieved what I had set out to do—to put an end to the harassment of the younger students—but not in the manner I had anticipated.

Reflecting on this incident, I realized I had not been very wise in my approach and had not given the matter adequate consideration; but I discovered more about my dedication to duty, and I secured a greater degree of respect from the students I had "rescued."

I learned many important lessons that year about loyalty,

leadership, and the motivation that is engendered by a belief in a cause. These feelings gained added dimension in my life when I joined the Church and became an advocate of the greatest of all causes—to declare principles of truth as they are so clearly defined by the gospel of Jesus Christ.

## SAFEGUARDING THE SABBATH

When I embarked on the previously mentioned business venture with Kenneth Warren, I left a secure position and moved into an environment of uncertainty. Kenneth was a man of integrity and industry, but we both recognized the vulnerability of our situation. We suddenly had to generate enough income every week to provide for ourselves and our families. To save expenses, we initially conducted our business out of our homes, which presented some challenges. I recall one incident that occurred on a Sunday morning.

Pamela and I were preparing to leave for church when the doorbell rang. I opened the door, and a man standing on the steps said, "I have purchased a car, and I need insurance. Can you help me?"

I explained that I would be more than happy to visit his home the following day to arrange the coverage, but unfortunately there was nothing I could do at that moment.

He responded, "But I have been referred to you and was told you could arrange insurance from your home."

I said, "That is true, but not on a Sunday."

He was becoming agitated and in sharper tones made it very clear that he needed insurance that very day. I apologized that I was not in a position to help and suggested that some service stations open on Sundays had the facility to furnish insurance. At that point he pulled from his pocket a handful of paper currency. Holding the notes out to me he said, "I have the money right here." Once more I apologized and offered my services as early as 5:00 A.M. the next day if that would help.

That was too much for him. "Well, that's ridiculous. You will not survive in business with that attitude. I'm a businessman myself and was considering giving you the opportunity to take care of all my insurance needs, but you can forget that!" He descended the steps leading to our home and headed off down the street. Pamela and I then left to attend Church services.

At 7:30 Monday morning, I was surprised when the man returned to my home. I invited him into the room I used as my office and provided him with a chair to sit on. He apologized for his impatience of the previous day and then said, "I was angry when I walked away from here yesterday, but when I reflected upon what you said, I concluded that I would want a man of integrity to take care of my insurance and that you were that man." It had been an easy decision not to transact business on the Sabbath because of my belief in a cause and my commitment to my covenants.

On other occasions, some of my business associates advised me that I could not afford to be totally honest in business, but this did not detract me from the principles I believed in or the promises I had made. Shakespeare gave utterance to a great truth when he had Polonius say: "This above all: to thine own self be true, And it must follow, as the night the day, Thou canst not then be false to any man" (*Hamlet*, Act I, Scene III).

As is the practice in business, I was sometimes invited to seminars and social functions where training was given and new products were introduced. The hosts of these events provided alcoholic beverages. My declining offers to drink sometimes caused my hosts some anxious moments. Several times, in the early days of my involvement, employees were hurriedly dispatched to purchase orange juice to accommodate what was to them my unusual behavior. I noted with interest over the years that more and more of those attending these functions expressed a preference for orange juice once it was made available.

We are often unaware of the impact our behavior can have on those with whom we associate or the influence for good that we can exert. I recall an occasion when a client submitted an insurance claim that appeared to be dubious. After satisfying myself that the claim was legitimate, I presented the claim form to the insurance company with my personal endorsement that this was a genuine circumstance, and I recommended that the claim be settled. An executive of the insurance company phoned me at my office and expressed doubts about the "improbable" reported loss but said he had authorized settlement on the basis of my endorsement.

Though personal gain should not be our aim, I have found that when I have been loyal to the gospel cause and honored my sacred covenants, things have ultimately worked in my favor. Bread cast on the water truly does ultimately return. My experience confirms what King Benjamin says in Mosiah 2:41: "Moreover, I would desire that ye should consider on the blessed and happy state of those that keep the commandments of God. For behold, they are blessed in all things, both temporal and spiritual; and if they hold out faithful to the end they are received into heaven, that thereby they may dwell in a state of never-ending happiness. O remember, remember that these things are true; for the Lord God hath spoken it."

## COMFORT THOSE WHO STAND IN NEED OF COMFORT

Another business-related experience taught me the importance of following righteous impulses. A few days before Christmas I learned that the eighteen-year-old daughter of one of our clients, whose business provided us with our greatest source of income, had been fatally injured in a motoring accident. I felt impressed to offer help by sharing my beliefs with him. He was already aware of my religious affiliation, but I thought he and his wife would be comforted if they understood our LDS view of mortality and the plan of salvation.

But I worried that my offer of help would be viewed as an inappropriate intrusion into their grief. Though I am not proud to admit it, I also feared offending him to the extent that it would put our business association in jeopardy. But then, like the prodigal son, "I came to myself" and concluded that whatever the outcome, I needed to act on the prompting I had felt.

In a telephone conversation, I extended to him my expressions of sympathy and asked if there was anything I could do to assist him and his family. He responded that there was nothing I could do and added that his greatest concern was for his wife, who was inconsolable and was spending most of her time in their bedroom trying to deal with her sorrow. Their priest had been to see her as had their physician, but she could not be comforted.

I felt I could help and pursued the matter by offering to visit their home. He initially resisted my suggestion but eventually agreed that I could do so with the understanding that his wife would probably not even leave the security of the bedroom to greet me. That didn't deter me, and, together with my business partner, I visited their home armed with a 16-millimeter film projector and a copy of *Man's Search for Happiness.*

The bereaved man greeted us on arrival and then retired to the bedroom to advise his wife that we had come to see her. After a time, he returned to the room in which we were waiting to say that he was not sure his wife would join us. Then my partner and I sat and listened as he described the circumstances of the accident in which their daughter had lost her life. She had lost control of her vehicle on black ice, and the car had left the road and collided with the trunk of a tree.

As we were visiting, his wife emerged from the bedroom displaying ample evidence of her distress. After I shared an insight into my feelings concerning the plan of salvation, we viewed together *Man's Search for Happiness.* The film opened the grieving parents' eyes to a concept they had never considered and helped plant a seed of hope in their hearts. Contemplating the possibility of life after death helped them begin the healing process.

We have so much to be grateful for in the truths revealed in the restoration of the gospel, and there are so many ways we can bring comfort to those who lack sufficient faith. At such times and in such moments, we can be the messengers of peace, particularly when we learn to recognize the voice of the Spirit and act when prompted to do so. Sensitivity to the Spirit is a gift that can be lost if it is not used. In the words of C. S. Lewis, "The more often a person feels without acting, the less he will be able ever to act, and, in the long run, the less he will be able to feel" (*The Screwtape Letters,* 1982, 61).

## STAND AS A WITNESS AT ALL TIMES

It is my observation that integrity, like other virtues, develops and flourishes when exercised, just as body muscles are strengthened through repeated use. Dr. Karl Maeser once said to a class of students, "Each one of you sooner or later must stand at the fork of the road and choose between personal interest and some principle of right." We will encounter continuing tests of our allegiance to the cause of truth and the covenants we have made, but each time we prevail, we grow in spiritual strength and moral character.

My appreciation for the progress we can make was highlighted in another experience associated with my business activity. A client for whom we managed a considerable insurance portfolio phoned to advise me that one of his trucks loaded with aluminum window frames had been stolen overnight. The load was valued at £16,000 ($24,000), in addition to the value of the vehicle. I invited him to my office so that we could complete the necessary paperwork in order to submit a claim to the insurance company.

He arrived at the office, and I began to ask him questions while completing the report. One condition of the insurance coverage was that loaded vehicles be secured in a compound or in a garage overnight. In response to a question about the vehicle's location, my client hesitated and then informed me that the vehicle had been parked in a lay-by (turnout) at the side of a highway. When I reminded him of the stipulation that the truck and load be properly secured, he wondered if there wasn't some way to make a claim anyway. He proposed a number of scenarios, but not one of the options he presented was feasible. Desperate to recoup his loss, he told me what a devastating effect the theft would have on his business. Wasn't there some way the insurance company could be influenced to pay his claim?

I sympathized with his plight and assured him that I would do everything within my power that was honorable to assist him. He was distraught and made it clear that if I was not able to arrange the settlement of his claim, he would be forced to withdraw his business from me and seek insurance elsewhere.

I didn't wish to lose his business, but to succumb to his propositions would have cost me my integrity, which was far more significant than a loss of money. There was no doubt in my mind as to what I could and could not do. I offered to speak by telephone to an executive of the insurance company, explain the circumstances, and inquire if he would be prepared to make a concession and consider settling the claim.

This proved to be unsuccessful, and the claim was declined. The client, who had been listening while I had the conversation, left my office in a rage, slamming the door behind him. I felt concern for him but also experienced an inner peace, knowing I had done the honorable thing.

A few days later, my client called me on the phone and expressed regret at the manner in which he had behaved. He asked if I would continue to manage his insurance for him, adding that he would not want the person who provided insurance for his company to be dishonest. We continued to take care of his insurance needs, and there was no animosity between us.

Earlier, in my quest for gospel understanding and in my attempts to apply Christian values to my business ventures, I might have debated what to do. But every honorable action taken and honest decision reached had helped refine my thinking and confirmed my resolve to do what I knew to be right.

## PRESS FORWARD WITH A PERFECT BRIGHTNESS OF HOPE

Looking back on our lives, we can all recall situations where we might have handled things differently or more wisely. One of those experiences in my life occurred when I was taking a driving test as a part of my application to obtain my British driving license.

At the direction of the examiner, I pulled out of the grounds where the test center was located and approached a set of traffic signals, where a red light was displayed. I stopped the vehicle and attempted to follow the procedures that I had practiced on so many occasions under the watchful eye of my driving instructor, Mr. Westhorpe.

But in the pressure of the moment, I overlooked a vital requirement. I had been taught that when stopping for a traffic signal to take the car out of gear and engage the hand brake. I had neglected to take the car out of gear, and when I let out the clutch, the car shuddered and stalled. It was an embarrassing moment, and I was convinced that it would result in my failing the test. However, I drove the remainder of the course with confidence and without making any more mistakes.

When we returned to the test center, the examiner commenced his evaluation by saying, "Mr. Johnson, you made a very serious mistake as you began the driving test, but you handled the car so well from then to the end of the drive that you restored my confidence in you as a competent driver." He then handed me the pink paper slip that indicated I had passed the test. I was surprised and elated.

This experience has a gospel parallel. When we make mistakes and when our performance is below what we know to be our best, we must exert every effort from that moment forward to do the best we can. If we do, a retroactive effect follows that can nullify the impact of our error. This power is manifest in the principle of repentance. When applied regularly in our lives, repentance permits us to move from weakness to strength, without the fear that our previous mistakes will disqualify us for the ultimate blessing of eternal life. Such is the graciousness of the Savior. We will be forever indebted to him for providing a way to overcome our weaknesses and be forgiven of our sins.

The lifestyle required of the Lord's disciples is seen by many in the world to be restrictive, to impose limitations that curtail personal freedom. In reality, the opposite is true. Commitment to a righteous cause and adherence to sacred covenants result in real freedom. The Savior himself confirmed this when he described his mission and the role his followers would play in it by saying, "For this cause came I into the world, that I should bear witness unto the truth" (John 18:37). He further declared, "If ye continue in my word, then are ye my disciples indeed; And ye shall know the truth, and the truth shall make you free" (John 8:31–32).

# ENTHUSIASTIC DEVOTION

## DISTINGUISHED BY ZEAL

For many years I have been fascinated by the description of the "people of Ammon." Alma 27:27 characterizes these remarkable people as being "distinguished for their zeal towards God, and also towards men; for they were perfectly honest and upright in all things; and they were firm in the faith of Christ, even unto the end."

A dictionary definition of the word *zeal* is "enthusiastic devotion." That is a thrilling description. Research into the word *enthusiasm* indicates the origin to be the Greek phrase *en theos*, which means "God within" or "the Spirit of God within."

We read in the Old Testament about a man called Caleb, one of twelve spies sent by Moses to reconnoiter the land of Canaan. Ten of the twelve returned from their mission with a negative report, detailing only the strength of its inhabitants, suggesting the impossibility of their overthrow. Only Joshua and Caleb had a different opinion. These two faithful men rent their clothes in a demonstration of their disdain for the others' report (see Numbers 14:6).

Caleb's enthusiasm for the task at hand is reflected in this description: "And Caleb stilled the people before Moses, and said, Let us go up at once, and possess it; for we are well able to overcome it" (Numbers 13:30). Rather than murmur against Moses and despair, as did the rest of Israel, Caleb and Joshua expressed their belief that "the Lord is with us" (Numbers 14:9).

The Lord recognized Caleb's faithfulness, declaring of him, "But my servant Caleb, *because he had another spirit with him*, and hath followed me fully, him will I bring into the land whereinto he went; and his seed shall possess it" (Numbers 14:24; emphasis added). The constancy of Joshua and Caleb is further verified in Numbers 32:11-12: "Surely none of the men that came up out of Egypt, from twenty years old and upward, shall see the land which I sware unto Abraham, unto Isaac, and unto Jacob; because they have not wholly followed me: save Caleb . . . and Joshua . . . *for they have wholly followed the Lord.*"

Later in his life, Caleb reflected on the events that had transpired and took comfort in his faithfulness: "Forty years old was I when Moses the servant of the Lord sent me from Kadesh-barnea to espy out the land: and I brought him word again as it was in mine heart. Nevertheless my brethren that went up with me made the heart of the people melt: *But I wholly followed the Lord my God.* And Moses sware on that day, saying, Surely the land whereon thy feet have trodden shall be thine inheritance, and thy children's for ever, *because thou hast wholly followed the Lord my God.*" We also learn that "Hebron therefore became the inheritance of Caleb . . . *because that he wholly followed the Lord God of Israel*" (Joshua 14:7-9, 14; emphasis added).

Caleb is a wonderful example of how the Spirit of the Lord can energize us and make us equal to the tasks that are laid upon us, regardless of their immensity. Enthusiastic devotion to the Lord's work is a wonderful credential and something I have admired in many members of the Church.

## ENTHUSIASM IS CONTAGIOUS

I found a shining example of someone who possessed a great power within in Elder Walt Stewart, who was assigned to supervise the construction of a chapel in my home city of Norwich, England. His tenacity and indomitable will became evident in something that happened during the completion of that project.

The brick masons had laid the inner wall breeze blocks almost to the full height of the building at the end that would house the cultural hall. The outer brickwork had been raised to approximately half of that height with a cavity left between the two layers for insulation. When the site was vacated one evening, all was well, but during the night an unusually strong wind raged through the area. By the following morning, what had stood as a majestic wall of brickwork and breeze blocks had been reduced to a pile of rubble.

The next morning when Walt arrived at the site with the Church building missionaries and brick masons, they surveyed a scene of devastation. Word of the calamity quickly spread, and members, particularly those who were providing volunteer labor, came to witness for themselves the extent of the damage. Amidst an air of gloom and despondency, a voice of optimism was heard as Walt Stewart began to rally the troops (he had been a U.S. Air Force hero during World War II) in a salvaging exercise.

It was winter and the high winds had been followed by a snowstorm and freezing temperatures. I vividly recall working one evening, side-by-side with my father-in-law, Thomas G. Wilson, by the glow of a light mounted on a wooden tripod. We were wrestling sections of blocks and bricks—still bonded together and frozen to the ground—into a position that would allow us to chip away the mortar and separate the bricks in an effort to salvage them for reuse. The headlight beam of a motorcycle pierced the darkness as a police constable pulled up to where we were working to investigate what we were doing. We had great difficulty convincing him that our activity was honorable; he was certain that only brick thieves would engage in such a pursuit under such conditions. Eventually, the police officer accepted the object of our efforts as honest.

Walt Stewart's vision and enthusiasm motivated an unusual effort to salvage as many of the building materials as possible. When the company that had supplied the brick learned of what had happened and that men, women, youth, and children were working to salvage the situation, they replaced the damaged bricks without charge. The salvaged bricks were then used as hard core for the floor base. What had initially been a calamity became a benefit, and members who had raised needed construction funds at great effort were able to complete the building without additional cost. William James, a sixteenth-century philosopher, observed that "the greatest discovery of this generation is that we can change our circumstances by changing our attitudes of mind." Like those described in the Book of Mormon, we can discover a power within us that, with nurturing, can develop into enthusiastic devotion.

## WHY NOT?

My understanding of the plan of salvation, which is also referred to as the great plan of happiness, produces feelings of great optimism in me. It causes me to view people and circumstances positively. It was George Bernard Shaw who said, "You see things; and you say, 'Why?' But I dream things that never were; and I say, 'Why not?'" (*Back to Methuselah* [1921], pt. I, act I.) Yes, we can change our circumstances by changing our attitudes, and a knowledge of who we are and of our potential as children of God can change our perspective. We can rise above obstacles and difficulties, building resistance and resilience to opposition, attaining the quality of character to act and not to be acted upon.

Joseph Smith observed, "Such was and always will be, the situation of the saints of God, that unless they have an actual knowledge that the course they are pursuing is according to the will of God they will grow weary in their minds and faint" (*Lectures on Faith,* Lecture 6, No. 4). Those who have developed the qualities of enthusiastic devotion manifest their attributes in many ways and under a variety of circumstances.

An experience in Iceland provides evidence of what can be accomplished by those who are not limited to what is normally accepted as man's capacities. In 1991 I was assigned to tour the Denmark Copenhagen Mission, which included visiting six missionaries and a couple serving the people of Iceland. Because of the complexity of the language, these missionaries spent their entire mission serving in one of the three branches of the Church located there. Spencer Greer was serving at that time as president of the mission, and he arranged to join me in a series of meetings with the missionaries, culminating in a district conference.

I noticed that a different elder played the piano for each hymn that was sung in the meetings. I was so impressed that there was so much talent among such a small group of missionaries that I expressed my feelings and made observations to this effect. President Greer asked what I was referring to specifically, and I told him how impressed I was that all of the missionaries could play the piano. The president paused, then explained that when he had received my letter prior to my visit outlining what I wanted to accomplish and suggesting the meetings that could be arranged, he had contacted the missionaries and suggested that it would be beneficial to have piano accompaniment for the singing of the hymns. Because none of the elders was an accomplished pianist, they decided that each of them would learn one hymn in preparation for the meeting. I was amazed and delighted to learn what they had been able to achieve on their Preparation day without taking time away from their missionary labors.

I further observed that during the closing hymn of the final meeting two missionaries sat at the piano. President Greer explained, "Well, that's a difficult hymn. One learned the bass and the other played the treble."

Through enthusiastic devotion, we can accomplish things that would otherwise not be considered possible and "dream of things that never were and ask why not." We can limit ourselves with the weight of low expectation or by wading through the mist of restricted vision. Those who wholly follow the Lord their God have a different Spirit in them, rise to greater heights of achievement, and develop deeper feelings of sensitivity to that which is divine.

## THE TYPHOON

On a different continent with a contrasting climate, I witnessed another impressive demonstration of enthusiastic devotion. I was attending the Mandaue Stake stake conference on the island of Cebu in the Philippines. President Lawrence A. Haines, the Cebu mission president, and his wife, Priscilla, provided accommodations and transportation to and from the stake center. A typhoon warning was in force, and on the Saturday afternoon of the conference weekend, ferocious winds and heavy rains struck the area. Only a few members made it to the chapel for the Saturday evening meeting. Power lines were down, and a portable generator was employed at the chapel to provide a reduced level of lighting and at least some amplification for the microphone. It was difficult conducting the meeting while trying to compete with the noise of the generator motor.

Following the meeting, President Haines provided transportation back to the mission home. It was extremely dark and difficult to find our way, the only light being that of the car headlights. At one point, we could see the lights of a vehicle traveling toward us, but they abruptly disappeared. We wondered what had happened to the approaching car, but in a moment we found out: the vehicle in which we were traveling was suddenly immersed in water that rose to the level of the windows. Water was surging across the road, and it was as though we were fording a river.

President Haines exclaimed, "We must keep moving!" After what were alarming moments, we emerged from the flow of rushing water and drove on, only to encounter a comparable situation farther along the road. After a harrowing journey, we eventually reached the safety of the mission home and spent the night protected from the storm.

The next morning blue skies and sunshine greeted us. As we drove to the chapel to attend the stake conference general session, we observed the debris, including fallen trees and stretches of standing water, which remained from the storm. In light of the severity of the gale and the effects of damage and flooding that were all about us, I asked President Haines if he thought many of the Saints would be able to make it to the meetings.

His response was, "Wait and see."

I was thrilled to see the Saints assemble, desiring to express their gratitude to the Lord for preserving and protecting them from the storm. A total of 453 people attended the meeting that day. As I sat on the stand preparing for the meeting, a counselor in the stake presidency approached me and apologized for wearing a wet shirt. I assured him that he needn't be concerned and said that I was pleased that he had made it to the meeting at all. He continued to apologize, explaining that his family home had been washed away with the floods the night before. He and his wife had searched the debris that morning, had found his white shirt, and had washed it by hand. He was sorry that it had not dried in time for the meeting.

After hearing his story, I thought of the environment in which I had been reared and of the abundance of material belongings I had learned to take for granted. Here was a brother who truly possessed enthusiastic devotion.

## AN ELEVATED PERSPECTIVE

Since I joined the Church, countless individuals and experiences have increased my appreciation for this significant and sacred quality of character. Enthusiastic devotion is inevitably manifest in acts of selfless service and evidences of dependability. I have concluded that, young or old, single or married, our highway of happiness is paved with acts of selfless service. One of the tragedies of life is that so many people believe that circumstances determine happiness. Of this notion, George Bernard Shaw observed: "People are always blaming their circumstances for what they are. I don't believe in circumstances. The people who get on in this world are the people who get up and look for the circumstances they want, and, if they can't find them, make them" (*Mrs. Warren's Profession* [1893], act II).

I believe there is a power within us, a divine heritage, which, when discovered, elevates our thoughts, improves our behavior, and expands our vision of what we may become. In the words of Samuel Johnson: "The fountain of content must spring up in the mind. He who has so little knowledge of human nature as to seek happiness by changing anything but his own disposition will waste his life in fruitless efforts and multiply the griefs he proposes to remove." In so saying, Johnson defined a great truth: We must begin with ourselves if we wish to be happy.

Enthusiastic devotion is the product of sustained faith in the Lord Jesus Christ and results in a continuing quest to attain the qualities of a righteous life. In truth, such enthusiastic devotion is also an expression of deep, abiding gratitude.

## LET YOUR HEARTS REJOICE

I have found that if we are to be truly happy, we must be enthusiastically devoted to some noble enterprise. Consider these stirring words: "Brethren, shall we not go on in so great a cause? Go forward and not backward. Courage, brethren; and on, on to the victory! Let your hearts rejoice, and be exceedingly glad. Let the earth break forth into singing. Let the dead speak forth anthems of eternal praise to the King Immanuel, who hath ordained, before the world was, that which would enable us to redeem them out of their prison; for the prisoners shall go free.

"Let the mountains shout for joy, and all ye valleys cry aloud; and all ye seas and dry lands tell the wonders of your Eternal King! And ye rivers, and brooks, and rills, flow down with gladness. Let the woods and all the trees of the field praise the Lord; and ye solid rocks weep for joy! And let the sun, moon, and the morning stars sing together, and let all the sons of God shout for joy! And let the eternal creations declare his name forever and ever! And again I say, how glorious is the voice we hear from heaven, proclaiming in our ears, glory, and salvation, and honor, and immortality, and eternal life; kingdoms, principalities, and powers!" (D&C 128:22–23). As Latter-day Saints, we certainly have reason to rejoice.

We read of many in holy writ who manifest these characteristics in their lives, and, in our day, President Gordon B. Hinckley radiates in his optimism and vision ample evidence of his enthusiastic devotion. This gift is not restricted, however, to office or ability. As President Hinckley has observed: "When there throbs in the heart of an individual Latter-day Saint a great and vital testimony of the truth of this work, he [or she] will be found doing their duty in the Church" (*Ensign,* May 1984, 99). This zeal is manifest in the lives of those who "wholly follow the Lord," for then they have another Spirit in them.

# DOCTRINES, PRINCIPLES, AND ORDINANCES

## ANCHORED TO TRUE DOCTRINE

We know what we should teach in the classroom and from the pulpit in Church meetings. This is clearly defined in the Doctrine and Covenants: "And I give unto you a commandment that you shall teach one another the doctrine of the kingdom. Teach ye diligently and my grace shall attend you, that you may be instructed more perfectly in theory, in principle, in doctrine, in the law of the gospel, in all things that pertain unto the kingdom of God, that are expedient for you to understand" (D&C 88:77-78). Our exemplar, Jesus Christ, provided us with a powerful pattern of how and what to teach.

We read in Mark 1:22: "And they were astonished at his doctrine: for he taught them as one that had authority and not as the scribes." The Savior possessed a unique ability to teach, which was noticeably more effective than the scribes or learned men at the time of his earthly ministry. The Savior's power as a teacher is also affirmed in Matthew 7:28-29: "And it came to pass, when Jesus had ended these sayings, the people were astonished at his doctrine: For he taught as one having authority [from God], and not as the scribes."

The use of the word *doctrine* is significant. In his marvelous experience in the Sacred Grove, young Joseph Smith was privileged to hear from the Savior's lips the Lord's evaluation of the preaching of men: "They draw near to me with their lips, but their hearts are far from me, they teach for doctrines the commandments of men, having a form of godliness, but they deny the power thereof" (JS–H 1:19). The philosophies of men pale beside the doctrines of heaven. According to Elder M. Russell Ballard, that great plan of happiness consists of doctrines—"infinite, eternal, absolute, unchanging principles" (*Ensign*, May 1995, 22).

Looking down through the ages to our day, the Apostle Paul made a great prophetic statement: "This know also, that in the last days perilous times shall come. For men shall be lovers of their own selves, covetous, boasters, proud, blasphemers, disobedient to parents, unthankful, unholy, Without natural affection, trucebreakers, false accusers, incontinent [lacking self-control], fierce, despisers of those that are good, Traitors, heady [rash, reckless], highminded [conceited], lovers of pleasures more than lovers of God." Moreover, the professors of man-made religion would be "ever learning, and never able to come to the knowledge of the truth." And they would have "a form of godliness; but [deny] the power thereof." These are timely warnings. Uninspired preachers and those who preach for gain are "evil men and seducers [who] shall wax worse and worse, deceiving, and being deceived." Paul's advice to Timothy was the same as the Savior's advice to Joseph Smith: "From such turn away" (2 Timothy 3:1–5, 7, 13).

We who have been introduced to the restored gospel of Jesus Christ are fortunate, indeed. We need not be "children, tossed to and fro, and carried about with every wind of doctrine, by the sleight of men, and cunning craftiness, whereby they lie in wait to deceive" (Ephesians 4:14).

Instead of depending for guidance on such, we are blessed to have the leadership of inspired Church leaders who teach revealed doctrines by the power of the Holy Spirit. These latter-day leaders are the equivalent of those described in the Book of Mormon: "They had waxed strong in the knowledge of the truth; for they were men of a sound understanding and they had searched the scriptures diligently, that they might know the word of God. But this is not all; they had given themselves to much prayer, and fasting; therefore they had the spirit of prophecy, and the spirit of revelation, and when they taught, they taught with power and authority of God" (Alma 17:2–3).

## DOCTRINE BRINGS STABILITY AMIDST STORMS

Once more I draw upon a personal experience to illustrate how having a grasp of true principles can help us avoid making critical mistakes.

In 1988 we decided to remodel our home by constructing additional bedroom space above the single-story living room, which had an existing flat roof. The builders set to work by first exposing the existing brickwork and laying courses of bricks until they had reached the required height. At this point they dismantled and removed the flat roof and suspended a sheet of tarpaulin over the exposed area to protect the ceiling and living room located below.

With our home thus exposed, I was awakened at about two o'clock the following morning by the sound of running water. I left our bedroom and descended the stairs to determine what was creating the sound. When I switched on the light in the living room, I was amazed to see water running from the light fixture that was suspended from the ceiling of the room. Outside, high winds and driving rain had dislodged the tarpaulin, and water was cascading over the upper side of the ceiling boards and had begun to penetrate into the living room.

I called to Pamela, and together we used cooking utensils, buckets, and towels, trying to contain the water and protect the carpet and furnishings from damage. It proved to be an impossible task as the deluge found its way through an increasing number of seams and joints in the exposed ceiling. Understandably, we did not sleep well for the few remaining hours until morning. Eventually the storm ceased, and after a time the stream of water diminished to a trickle and then a drip. By then, the carpet was wet, the ceiling boards also; but, fortunately, we had been able to protect the furniture and other items in the room.

At 9:00 A.M. I phoned the insurance company, which immediately instructed a loss adjuster to come and inspect the damage. He arrived midmorning and following a brief inspection, contacted a company that specialized in drying and cleaning carpets in circumstances such as these. As we were filling out the insurance forms and discussing the redecoration that would be necessary, I was perplexed by an observation the adjuster made.

"You could have prevented much of this damage!" he said.

Feeling we had done all that we could have under the circumstances, I asked what he meant. He explained that had I but made a hole in the ceiling in the area where the water first penetrated, it would have flowed to this point and could have easily been collected in containers, thus preventing damage to the paint work on the walls and the wide expanse of carpet.

Had we been aware of what to do, we might have saved ourselves the exhausting activity of that night, and we would not have had to rush about, responding frantically to each new stream of water that appeared.

## THE SCRIPTURES: A SOURCE OF DOCTRINE

The doctrine of the gospel of Jesus Christ provides us with an awareness of the purpose of life and how to govern ourselves. It is the doctrine that keeps us from being "tossed to and fro" and from being deceived "by the sleight of men, *and* cunning craftiness, whereby they lie in wait to deceive" (Ephesians 4:14). Paul provides additional instruction on how to guard against deception: "But continue thou in the things which thou hast learned and hast been assured of, knowing of whom thou hast learned them; And that from a child thou hast known the holy scriptures, which are able to make thee wise unto salvation through faith which is in Christ Jesus" (2 Timothy 3:14-15).

In the words of Elder Boyd K. Packer, "The scriptures provide the pattern and the basis for correct doctrine. From doctrine, we learn principles of conduct" (*Ensign*, May 1994, 20). Paul continues: "All scripture is given by inspiration of God, and is profitable for doctrine, for reproof, for correction, for instruction in righteousness: That the man of God may be perfect, throughly furnished unto all good works" (2 Timothy 3:16-17). The remedy for erroneous ethics, false philosophies, and marginal morality is correct doctrine derived from the divine source. Doctrine provides a constant to which we can cling amidst raging storms of conflicting opinions that can otherwise stir up anger and animosity.

## GROUNDED IN SOUND DOCTRINE

For seeds to flourish and grow, they need to be sewn in fertile soil. When visiting Iceland in 1991, I was surprised to see on the drive from the airport to Reykjavik a terrain devoid of trees and foliage. The landscape consisted of a rocky surface covered only by a green, moss-like growth. Our driver explained that the birchwood trees that had originally grown in this area had been cut to obtain timber. Extensive grazing and lava flows had also combined to virtually eliminate the fertile earth in which plant life might have flourished. As we approached the community, he pointed out areas where trees, bushes, and plant life were growing, adding that topsoil had been shipped in to make this possible.

Just as plant life grows in fertile soil, so true principles have their root in correct doctrine. Application of true principles brings success in every field of righteous endeavor and personal behavior.

King Benjamin was an effective teacher whose words had a powerful effect on his listeners. Following one of his sermons, his listeners "all cried with one voice, saying: Yea, we believe all the words which thou hast spoken unto us; and also, we know of their surety and truth, because of the Spirit of the Lord Omnipotent, which has wrought a mighty change in us, or in our hearts, that we have no more disposition to do evil, but to do good continually" (Mosiah 5:1-2).

This was such a remarkable response that I wished to explore further the content of King Benjamin's message. In Mosiah 2:9, King Benjamin prefaced his sermon by saying: "I have not commanded you to come up hither to trifle with the words which I shall speak, but that you should hearken unto me, and open your ears that ye may hear, and your hearts that ye may understand, and your minds that the mysteries of God may be unfolded to your view." From this powerful opening statement to the unanimous acceptance of the people, King Benjamin taught the people doctrine and principles, confirming again what Elder Packer has said: "True doctrine, understood, changes attitudes and behavior" (*Ensign,* November 1986, 17). That is the kind of teaching that has the power to bring about a mighty change of heart.

## "AS THE DEWS FROM HEAVEN"

The Lord has instructed us how to prepare ourselves to be effective teachers of the word: "Let thy bowels also be full of charity towards all men, and to the household of faith, and let virtue garnish thy thoughts unceasingly; then shall thy confidence wax strong in the presence of God; and the *doctrine* of the priesthood shall distil upon thy soul as the dews from Heaven." If we are thus prepared, "The Holy Ghost shall be [our] constant companion" (D&C 121:45-46) and "shall teach [us] all things" (John 14:26).

The words of a favorite hymn describe poetically this cycle of learning:

> *As the dew from heav'n distilling*
> *Gently on the grass descends*
> *And revives it, thus fulfilling*
> *What thy providence intends,*
> *Let thy doctrine, Lord, so gracious,*
> *Thus descending from above,*
> *Blest by thee, prove efficacious*
> *To fulfill thy work of love.*
> (Hymns, *no. 149*)

Our faith and hope are revived by divine doctrine as it distills upon our hearts and minds.

Following my baptism and confirmation, Pamela's father nurtured my developing testimony as I accompanied him as a home teaching companion. He not only taught me how to be an effective home teacher but explained also the principles of priesthood and Church government that underlie the service we give in the Church. I constantly reflect on the lessons he taught me and the example he provided, all of which helped to establish the foundation of my faith.

## THE POWER OF GODLINESS

Earlier in this chapter, I referred to the power of godliness. What is this power and how is it manifest? D&C 84:20-21 provides the answer: "Therefore, in the ordinances [of the Melchizedek priesthood], the power of godliness is manifest. And without the ordinances thereof, and the authority of the priesthood, the power of godliness is not manifest unto men in the flesh." Of these principles, the Prophet Joseph Smith taught: "The ordinances of the Gospel . . . were laid out before the foundations of the world" (*Teachings of the Prophet Joseph Smith*, 367). That is one of the things that originally attracted me to the message of the Restoration: the doctrine is not to be altered or changed. All must be saved on the same basis—"by obedience to the laws and ordinances of the Gospel" (Article of Faith 3).

These truths were revealed first to Adam, of whom we read: "And thus the Gospel began to be preached, from the beginning, being declared by holy angels sent forth from the presence of God, and by his own voice, and by the gift of the Holy Ghost. And thus all things were confirmed unto Adam, by an holy ordinance, and the Gospel preached, and a decree sent forth, that it should be in the world, until the end thereof; and thus it was. Amen" (Moses 5:58-59).

The importance of ordinances is confirmed by the word of the Lord: "And again, I will give unto you a pattern in all things, that ye may not be deceived . . . Wherefore he that prayeth, whose spirit is contrite, the same is accepted of me if he obey mine ordinances" (D&C 52:14-15).

Participating in ordinances and making covenants is essential if we hope to avoid deception, live in harmony with and be nurtured by true points of doctrine, and be assured that "whoso treasureth up my word, shall not be deceived" (JS—M 1:37).

## "TAKE HEED UNTO THYSELF"

The counsel given by the Apostle Paul to Timothy describes the pattern that holds the key to personal discovery and individual testimony: "Meditate upon these things; give thyself wholly to them; that thy profiting may appear to all. Take heed unto thyself, and unto the doctrine; continue in them: for in doing this thou shalt both save thyself, and them that hear thee" (1 Timothy 4:15-16).

The last line of the hymn "Reverently and Meekly Now" has special significance to me. It reads, "And be constant unto me, That thy Savior I may be" (*Hymns*, no. 185).

I am striving to obtain this quality of constancy unto the Lord, that the name *Savior* might not simply be a title to which I refer but that the full extent of the Atonement might be efficacious in my life and in the lives of those whom I love. May it be efficacious in your life as well.

# INDEX